THE SINGER I'LL LOVE FOR THE SONG

Sing me a song with the ring of the truth in it,
Sing me a song with the freshness of youth in it,
Chant me a paean of joy.
I am tired of the dirge with regrets and despair in it,
Life has too much of drab sorrow and care in it,
Raise me a chorus with hopefulness rare in it,
Plucked from the heart of a boy.
Give me the splash and the shout of the sea in it,
The trebles of birds and the bass of the bee in it,
Bring the Spring's minstrels along,
Trilling a lay with the zest of young life in it,
Tender and clean with no heartache of strife in it;
Sing me a message with joyfulness rife in it,
And the singer I'll love for the song.

(From 'The Parish of St Mel's', John O'Brien)

This book has been written and published to mark the Australian celebration of the centenary of the death of Saint John Bosco.

THE SINGER I'LL LOVE FOR THE SONG

Reflections for Parents & Teachers

JULIAN FOX S.D.B.

Collins Dove

Published by COLLINS DOVE
60-64 Railway Road, Blackburn, Victoria 3130
Telephone (03) 877 1333

Designed by Mary Goodburn
Typeset in Vladimir by Solo Typesetting, South Australia
Printed by The Book Printer, Victoria

National Library of Australia
Cataloguing-in-Publication data:

Fox, Julian, S.D.B.
    The singer I'll love for the song.

    ISBN 0 85924 702 3.

    1. Christian education of children.
    2. Christian education of young people.
    3. Church and education. 4. Catholic Church
    – Education. I. Title.

200'.7'i

Contents

Introduction

It is something of an irony that I found myself in Rome precisely at the time that Pope John Paul II was in Australia. Rome has a pleasant climate, even in late October and early November – 'le ottobratte' the Romans call this time of warmth and maturity, and I struck the warmest and longest Autumn since the war – but it is not Australia! I could not but help think of the Pope in Sydney, at the massed gathering there, or with the young unemployed in Hobart, or the even younger grade four class in Melbourne, and feel anew a yearning for the young people of Australia. The purpose of my visit to Rome, however, was to share with Salesians from all around the globe, and to learn from them. It has been enriching for me to have realized that, despite the marked contrast between the conditions of the young in Maputo (Mozambique) and Melbourne, the heart of my Salesian brother Francisco beats with the same yearning. It is the young we love, whoever they are, wherever they are.

My thoughts turned to Spring, back home, and the words of one John O'Brien. His name was really Father Patrick Hartigan. Writing in the 1930s while parish priest of Narrandera (N.S.W.), he was not to know that nearly sixty years later, Pope John Paul II would say to the young people of the world:

Everywhere I have met young people thirsty for love and for truth . . . In you there is hope, for you belong to the future, just as the future belongs to you.

I have always enjoyed the poetry of John O'Brien, but one poem in particular struck me forcibly in the light of the Pope's words. Here, so far from Australian shores, it took on a profound meaning for me:

Sing me a song with the ring of the truth in it,
Sing me a song with the freshness of youth in it,
Chant me a paean of joy.

1

I am tired of the dirge with regrets and despair in it,
Life has too much of drab sorrow and care in it,
Raise me a chorus with hopefulness rare in it,
Plucked from the heart of a boy.
Give me the splash and the shout of the sea in it,
The trebles of birds and the bass of the bee in it,
Bring the Spring's minstrels along,
Trilling a lay with the zest of young life in it,
Tender and clean with no heartache of strife in it;
Sing me a message with joyfulness rife in it,
And the singer I'll love for the song.

(From 'The Parish of St Mel's', John O'Brien)

Over many years, working amongst young people, I have, I believe, heard the chorus which John O'Brien imagines. More often than not, this chorus has been 'plucked from the heart of a boy' simply because my experience has been largely amongst boys. In writing for them, their parents and their teachers, as has been my wont, I have been attempting to express something of the charism of St John Bosco, better known simply as Don Bosco, founder of the Salesians. Joy, for Don Bosco, was the eleventh commandment, and one of the great secrets of his 'Preventive System'. Young people, he was convinced, were naturally joyful and they shared, in addition, the other virtues that one finds in the quoted verse of John O'Brien: truth, hope, and a zest for life. Don Bosco's saintly genius was to be able to recognize these virtues in the words and actions of the young.

While this book is not a text on Don Bosco's Preventive System, I hope it reflects the style of education which underpins that system. It is a style more caught than taught, more to be described than prescribed. In effect, it is a tune to be hummed because it is catchy. Behind it lies the singer, for the method of Don Bosco was more interested in the singer than the tune.

Moments have sizes, and tunes have their moods. Nor do the moments follow one another in strict order. This is not a book to be read cover to cover as if the last chapter is an important product of the first. Choose your song according to mood. My only wish is that you, too, discover the singer.

It must be recognized, too, that the genesis of these pages has been in the many pastoral bulletins I have written over the years for school staffs, parents, and sometimes for the youngsters themselves. They were never meant to be read in sequence, nor, in some cases, out of context. I have looked long and hard through every bookshop that has come my way, for something that would help a principal, who feels very deeply his pastoral role, write for his educative community. By this term I mean all who are in that community. I found very little to help me, and it is in the hope that this book will help not only principals, but all who are involved with Catholic education, that I have written it. 'Collated it', might be more accurate. It is no 'opera' in any sense of that word. At best it may be a medley; but then, medleys have a way of being 'listenable' that operas don't! If nothing else, it reminded me joyfully of 'Spring's minstrels . . .', while gathering swallows here have been twittering in the skies.

Julian Fox S.D.B.
Rome, December 1986

PART ONE

A shepherd's pastorale

The pastorale, the dictionary tells us, is a quietly flowing instrumental composition with notes flowing in groups of three. What better symbol could there be to set the mood for a description of 'Youth Pastoral', a term that is unusual in English, but richer than 'Youth Ministry' in intent. Youth Pastoral is the Church's presence amongst the young, be it the charismatic influence of a John Paul II, the systematic promotion of parish youth activity, or that style which followers of Don Bosco know simply as a triad of Reason–Religion–Lovingkindness.

'And what do you want to do for a living?'

'And what do you want to do for a living?' It seems a normal enough question. It would seem, indeed, to be the goal of most young people to be able to answer it one day, and a casual exchange with any parent or teacher will indicate that it rates high on their list of priorities, too.

So, let's try some responses: 'Think I'll be an under-taker'. Gasp! (not for too long, or you will be in need of one). Or, 'I'm going to be an entree . . . er, an en tout . . . er, an entrepreneur'. Good lad. Bob Ansett will be proud of you (and here is a copy of the *New Syllabus Speller* to help you on your way). Or, 'I want to be a politician'. But the question, my friend, was what you were going to *do* for a living!

There's the rub. For a simple question it seems to have a complicated answer. How does one explain a priest-principal? 'I'm a hyphenated priest.' Gasp! Is it contagious? Forget trying to explain what a principal does. No one, not even a principal, can adequately describe that. So, let's drop the hyphen for the moment. I am a priest, for young people, for everybody. I write birthday letters after break-fast, play handball at recess and cadge licorice sticks from kindly mothers or sycophantic seniors in the tuckshop. Now that sounds daft and decidedly secular. I should also say that I pray (before breakfast if the flesh is not weak), celebrate the Eucharist ... but, you query, are praying and celebrating *doing*?

It must be obvious. The question was wrong from the outset. A priest, a principal, a politician, an undertaker – it's not what they do but what they are that matters. Each has a special quality of presence to the world and to other human beings. I have decided anyway, that praying belongs to my quality as a human being even before it belongs to my quality as a priest. It is not something I do, but something I am: a quality of presence to myself first, then to God, then to others. Does that order look strange? Being it in any other sequence sends me the wrong way up the entrance to the freeway of life.

To be a priest is to tackle a challenging and exciting kind of presence – of being. Some of those dreadful ads for the priesthood or religious life try to tell you what you will do. It is a bit like the descriptions I recall hearing in primary school of what heaven would be like. In terms of the 'doings' that were offered I preferred, even then, hanging around tuckshops sucking lollipops to the likelihood of a golden glimpse of the Almighty from a heavenly hurdy-gurdy.

Let me tell you that my experience of being a priest, and a Salesian to boot, does not make me feel guilty about the lollipops or the licorice sticks, not even the unashamed cadging. Not if it means a quality of presence to someone. It has its spiritual quality too, sometimes very pronounced like the time someone turned up – a young being for whom life was pressure, not presence – and simply said: 'Father, I want to go to confession . . .'. Now, those few moments of presence would have been worth a thousand cadgings. I would have cadged a licorice stick from Old Nick for the privilege.

I have been using the priesthood because that is my experience of who I am rather than what I do. Were I simply to list what I do, it might suggest that God's call is limited to very few, perhaps those with the intellectual equipment, as in the case of one studying to be a doctor or a lawyer. But to consider what a priest or religious is – a quality of presence to self, God, others – is to suggest that very many potentially have the call. I certainly see many young people who are a quality presence to their companions. Should they not be prepared to admit, or should not others be prepared to help them admit that God may desire them to continue that presence as a specific calling in life?

Being attentive to the song in order to know the singer requires a presence. Many of the letters and articles that make up this collection deal with that presence, as I have understood it. And of one thing I am certain. 'Being' a priest and Salesian has been an utter joy. 'Doing' the job has had its awkward moments. But I think that has a precedent, don't you? Being the Son of God meant, for Jesus, dwelling in eternal love: 'This is my Beloved Son . . .' (Matthew 3:17). Doing it amongst thieves and murderers brought him to a sticky end – for three days only!

The Lord be with you

Perhaps it is a weakness of language teachers to be interested in little words; perhaps it is also their strength that they are unhappy with slapdash communication. Prepositions are small words in most languages but, from my experience of learning foreign languages, they give the learner a problem that belies their size! English speakers, unconfined by case for the most part, may even overlook the force of the prepositions they use. Centuries ago, the Christian world worried certain prepositions as a dog will worry a bone; East and West divided over the expression of the relationship of Spirit to Father and Son . . . and it all hinged on the force of certain prepositions: 'through' or 'from' whom? I would like to spend some time with a sentence which is much more taken for granted than that troublesome sentence from antiquity, yet I believe it also needs worrying.

'The Lord be with you.' There, in a single expression, is a whole theology, but also a whole educational method and a way to holiness, and it stems from a simple preposition.

We may begin from experience first of all. God is often felt to be the one 'beyond'. Even in more common language we may use the expression 'Lord above!' At a more technical level, scholars have argued whether John's Gospel offers a view of Christ 'from above' or 'from below' – is Jesus the eternal Logos dwelling with the Father from all eternity ('from above' theology) or is he the man taken over by the Spirit of God at his baptism ('from below' theology)? It is so easy to become embroiled in this 'above–below' thinking that it affects the way we think of the whole New Testament and its central revelation: the Word became Flesh and dwelt amongst us. While scholars may debate the 'above–below' implications of such a revelation, I am more interested in the fact that God is *with* us. 'Where two or more are gathered in my name . . .' (Matthew 18:20). In the Christian mystery we are caught up into the relationship with the divine presence in our midst. I put it to you that if 'with you' was good enough for the Lord, then it must be good enough for us, for anyone who is in his Church and is attempting to carry out his mission.

This is my starting point. *Being with* seems to be the simple, central tenet of the Gospel's revelation. And if the life of Jesus of Nazareth is the ultimate norm for those who would proclaim his way, then *being with* is something new – a way of doing things that has challenged the world. If you examine Jesus' Way and his teaching, his style and content, you will discover that it is new and is recognized as such.

But we haven't gone nearly far enough. *Being with* does not fully encompass the nature of Jesus' presence and its newness. It was in fact a *being with for* – for us and for our salvation. At the centre of the eucharistic act we find this reminder. Jesus' *being with* was not static, but something that either drove him to others or vitally attracted them to him. Jesus' *being with* reached out towards others. Its best image in those days was the *being with for* of the shepherd. A visit to the Roman catacombs offers the evidence for this image – Jesus the Good Shepherd is depicted everywhere. Hence the word 'pastoral'. Jesus' love and style of presence came to be known as pastoral love with a distinctive presence that humankind had not known before.

Is it any wonder that the early Fathers of the Church, seeking a word to describe Jesus, other than by the image I have just referred to, use the word *paidagogos* – the pedagogue being the one who accompanied a youngster from home to wherever – through the city streets – usually to school. Pedagogy has its roots right there in the *being with for* of that image. This, I would suggest, is to be at the heart of the personal approach of teacher, parent, guardian: the way Jesus did it.

The logic of Christian education in this understanding is as follows:

1   Those who would educate or nurture in the name of Christ will claim Christ as their model.

2   To know Christ, however, to really know him, is to know him as one sent from above, or as one to whom we unworthily relate from below, but as one who is intimate. 'I live now, not I, but Christ lives in me', said Paul (Galatians 2:20). Jesus is the one who is with us for our salvation and who reveals a God who is with us for our salvation. He offered intimacy with himself and God.

3   If we know him this way then we, like him, are impelled to be for others for their salvation. If we really are as Christ, then the whole world craves his companionship in us. So, pastoral charity is the content and method of our approach.

When an educator like Don Bosco is remembered for saying something so seemingly commonplace as: 'Here among you I feel happy; this is how I want to spend my life, in your midst' (Biographical Memoirs IV, 455), then from the reasoning above we can see that the Gospel is being proclaimed. And we can understand why unlearned and unloved youngsters, whose culture was not saying anything like that to them, felt attracted to the man and ultimately to the One whose love he was representing.

And today's culture? It, too, does not say anything like that to today's young people. The task is ours – to be happy in their midst.

Let us love as Jesus loved

'Eunuch' was as barbed a label in Pilate's Palestine as 'pansy' is for us today. The evidence suggests Jesus was fair game for ridicule in the matter of his companionship and style of presence. And yet, if we accept the centrality of love to Jesus' message and way of life, we have to see that he was not addressing his words and actions to engaged or married people alone – not even primarily. To argue that the cultural scene in Jesus' time allowed him to say directly to his followers: 'Love one another as I have loved you' (John 15:12), would be to miss the point as well as to be inaccurate. Of course, we still repeat that phrase, and think nothing of it. After two thousand years of repetition, it may have lost its force. But nineteen centuries later, Don Bosco was to say to his followers: '. . . the youngsters should not only be loved, but they themselves should know that they are loved . . . Affection is our rule of life' (from the 'Letter from Rome' quoted in Appendix to *Salesian Constitutions*) Don Bosco told his early Salesians. The question is, how do we demonstrate our love and show our affection in a society which has seemingly lost the force of the concept, or worse, has demeaned it?

The phrase 'I love you' is hardly one to be heard around school-yards or classrooms. It has a rather restricted context. The three word surface structure would imply a deeper structure which seems appropriate only in the context of actual or intended marital partnership. While being conscious of what one can or cannot realistically say in contexts that are generally accepted, I would like to place the command 'love as Jesus loved' in its wider Christian context.

If love is relegated to the left hemisphere of the brain, that part now understood to be the domain of analytical thinking, the strength of the Christian message is diminished. Jesus said, quoting the well-known Shema, that we must love with our whole heart, mind, soul and strength. And in the Christian tradition, men and women have loved passionately in both married and celibate contexts. It suffices to read the letters that ran between St Francis de Sales and St Jane-Frances de Chantal to see this.

There is something poignant about many of the statues depicting Don Bosco, particularly the one that stands directly above St Peter, near the High Altar in St Peter's

Basilica, Rome. It is not Don Bosco alone who is depicted, but Don Bosco with his hand resting on the shoulder of a boy. Neither the twentieth century, nor a strongly macho Australian culture, should prevent us, too, from expressing our love through word and gesture, and forcefully, according to the principles of the Gospel. I believe there are things we can be especially clear about in our Christian relationships.

I have already written briefly of the background to the word 'pedagogy'. The *paidagogos*, in Greek culture, was the family servant who, from a child's earliest years, took him in charge, accompanied him through the city streets, helped him live in his environment through advice, example and help with decision-making. The function was not primarily academic. The servant and child formed a relationship that drew on the affective resources of both – not without attendant dangers. But so powerful was the image of the pedagogue thus understood, that the early Fathers would often describe Jesus as the 'companion educator' of the Christian.

The 'companion educator' is a concept that I find attractive and helpful. We need to rise above the eroticized culture of our times which would want to restrict our range of feelings to a single focus, that which we call 'romantic'. As companion educators, especially in the style of affection that Don Bosco practised, we say to the young in word and action that we enjoy their presence, appreciate their being, and care enough to do what is really worthwhile for them. That is the level at which the Good Samaritan acted when he physically lifted up the beaten Jew. That is the level at which Jesus acted when the Gospel tells us that he looked steadily at the rich young man 'and loved him' (Mark 10:21), or when he took the little children, 'put his arms around them, laid his hands on them and gave them his blessing' (Mark 9:36).

'If you want to be loved, you must make it clear that you love' (from the 'Letter from Rome' quoted in Appendix to *Salesian Constitutions*). So said Don Bosco. In no sense is this love a dominating love. Too many people have been loved in the name of Christ, regardless of their complete indifference to the fact! That is not the way of Don Bosco. He loved in order to create the desire to love in return, and his model was Jesus. Both divine and human love are marked by mutuality. The specifically Christian revelation about love is just this – that we have been loved, so loved in fact, that our sins are forgiven. The full realization of that fact produces a powerful feeling of love. Witness Mary Magdalen at the feet of Jesus. Could it be that often we are so busy showing our love that we have little time to accept it in return? Especially where the young are concerned, we need to know how to read the little signs that are their response of confidence and love.

There is one final thought that comes from my experience as an educator, and perhaps applies more to the school context than elsewhere. Individuals always felt individually loved and regarded in Don Bosco's 'family', but it is also true that the one-to-one mutuality of this love was expressed in the context of the group. I believe we should not overlook this. We like to see our pupils actively involved in their games, or in the classroom, or gathered in groups. Our pupils also like us to see them that way. I think that we get to love them and to express our love for them especially in that context. This safeguards our expression of affection, ensuring on the one hand that it does not go astray, and on the other, that it is not misinterpreted. For, after all, to love as Jesus loved is to love without the exclusion of others. John the Beloved was no isolated pet – he was just more open to receiving the same love that had been bestowed on Judas.

Let us try to love as Jesus loved.

Don Bosco's triad

These first chapters all bear the unmistakable imprint of Don Bosco. And while I have said initially that it is not my intention to write a textbook on the Preventive System, an explanation of that term is at least warranted. It is his own phrase for an educational practice based on the triad of reason, religion and lovingkindness. It is a triad that has been worked into a symphony, and played for the greater glory of God and the salvation of souls.

Don Bosco's educational practice is outlined in a small treatise which he wrote after many requests. It is a treatise (simply called *The Preventive System*) which, on its own, may not respond adequately to precise questions of educational philosophy or classroom technique; it was not meant to prescribe details of that kind, but to describe an attitude that could underpin them. Don Bosco's explanation is fundamentally theological. He says this quite explicitly. He had his techniques, but these are no better nor worse than other techniques unless vivified by the attitudes underlying them. You can trace Don Bosco's ideas on classroom techniques to the De La Salle Brothers of Turin, amongst others. He did not claim that his 'system' was a unique way to teach; he does seem to claim that it is a unique way of educating, however, and I offer these thoughts to all who are in a position of assisting the young to grow, in life and the love of God.

There may be an astonishing variety of approach and practice adopted by those who would educate as Don Bosco did, but all share a common factor – the educator must be observably 'a sign and bearer of the love of God for the young' (*Salesian Constitution* No. 2). One of the most consoling facts of Christian theology is that we are present to God as individuals. We are known and loved by God for what we are, as we are. In Don Bosco's approach we aim at being the messenger, the vehicle, the embodiment of this personal love.

The basic principle, the *sine qua non* of the system, then, is attentive loving presence going back to the way Christ lived amongst mankind. It follows that the more committed we are to Christ and his way of life, the more perfect will be our application of the system. There is only one way this sort of relationship can be established: the constant, actual, friendly presence of the educator. Don Bosco worked 'from the inside', so to speak.

One has a choice of working from the outside or from the inside. The former approach means to contain the group so that some sort of educational process takes place, but leaving the efficacy of that process to either good will or coercion. Don Bosco points out that this works well with adults of good will, or in the army. The educator is certainly not precluded from being benevolent in such an approach, but is more likely to remain aloof in the belief that this allows for the freedom of the individual to respond or not.

On the other hand, the technique of working from the inside demands more than benevolence; it demands a certain sympathy. It demands being with the youngster in every aspect of his life, sharing it and liking it, all the time as an adult committed Christian. We can work and sacrifice ourselves to the point of death, Don Bosco declares in a letter he wrote to his Salesians from Rome, 'but it is not enough: the best thing is missing' (ibid). And what is the best thing? 'That the boys not only be loved, but they should realize they are loved' (ibid). It is not an approach to be taken unreflectively. Let me put it this way: the kindness which Don Bosco regarded as essential to education has no connection with mere sentiment. It is not an easy condescension, blind to the shortcomings of the young. Rather is it a judicial combination of gentleness and strength, indulgence and firmness, in which strictness and consideration, determination and patience, are justly poised. A tall order? Not with the help of God.

Don Bosco did not believe in great insistence on authority. Gaining ascendency over the hearts of the young was fundamental to his system, but this was to be achieved by a winning manner and through the persuasion of their own reason. He disapproved of orders given with threats, of harsh, biting or sarcastic remarks, and of public punishments. On the other hand he condemned equally those who, through timidity or weakness, allowed the boys to do what they liked. He frequently reminded educators that the power of good example was one of the strongest instruments for good.

Don Bosco recognized the need for occasional punishments, but it was his desire that they be avoided as far as possible. Why is punishment inflicted? To correct the offender or to serve as an example to others. When there is no need to make an example, and when there are other means for securing the end in view, those means should be employed, even though they entail effort on the part of the educator.

Does this system form character? Don Bosco realized that strong characters are not formed by external pressure but by inward conviction, by dint of numerous sacrifices, and of sacrifices willingly undergone. Kindness alone induces young people to make the sacrifices and undergo the struggles necessary to form character. Don Bosco insisted on order, discipline, constant application to work, devotion to duty, and the correction of defects, all of which requires continuous effort.

The meeting that takes place between a young person and the adult who bears responsibility for education is a kind of proposal. I have often put it this way when accepting new students into school. Anton Chekhov wrote a short play called *The Proposal*. For him, the proposal is beset by human limitation, a missing of the mark. While not accepting his viewpoint entirely, I accept that a proposal has a strong element of risk in it, and that this is what happens in the meeting between two freedoms, as occurs in the educational relationship between educator and educand. Let me put it this way:

1 As a specifically Christian proposal, we are offering our belief that God loves people and that this can be discovered in the person of Christ. This is made explicit in a programme of religious education.

2 Proposals are best made personally. To the extent that we develop techniques which make education personal, we are likely to elicit a personal response.

3 A proposal that addresses one's whole life has more chance of acceptance than one which does not. Hence Don Bosco was interested in not only good Christians, but also honest citizens.

4 A proposal is only a beginning. It must allow for growth.

5 A proposal is an invitation to partnership and accompaniment. It assumes presence and an enlivening, personal relationship.

6 No proposal is really a proposal if it is enforced. Ultimately we have to live with the educational risk that what we offer may be freely rejected.

Magnificat

As thousands of youngsters all over the countryside have always known, faith and life are fused on the football ground . . . real life and real faith, which can sustain the occasional heresy of 'Our Lady wallops Sacred Heart' or 'Fatima fixes Corpus Christi – by four points!' As the victors sing their own little 'magnificats' after the match little do they realize that 'Our Lady' who nurtures them and their game, win or lose, herself scored a four-point victory on 29 October 1963. That was the day the Bishops voted at Vatican II to resolve the centuries of tension between those who would put her above the Church or as an appendix to it. Mary must have sung her own Magnificat once more as she found herself squarely amidst the Church, in chapter VIII (*Lumen Gentium*).

It may be at Mum's knees that most of us first learned to greet the Mother of God, but I have no doubt that it is the Catholic school which kept that fervour alive. It is fitting that Mary should have been so aligned with education in the faith and education for life. In the past the religious did their job extraordinarily well, bringing to faith and life their own Marian tradition. Hopefully they continue to do so, but at a time when numbers of religious are fewer amongst Catholic teachers, it would be a tragedy if the role that Mary plays in the life of young believers were to also diminish. Now that theology has found the balance in Mary's regard, it would be unfortunate if Catholic educational practice were to lose it.

Education according to the spirit and method of Don Bosco would be impoverished without Mary. Since the spirit and the method are open to anyone who wishes to read the Gospel along the lines traced out by Don Bosco, I offer the following thoughts as a way of ensuring Mary a place in our accompaniment of the young.

He began his work of catechesis with a 'Hail Mary' on 8 December 1841. Some seventeen years before that, at the age of nine, Don Bosco dreamt he was in a large playing field amidst a wild group of boys, when a majestic Lady appeared to him (accompanied by a noble Man) and confirmed this would be the field of his life's labour as well as indicating the method by which he would work. In more than a dozen dreams after that, Don Bosco saw and was instructed by a figure he recognized as Mary.

Was Don Bosco a dreamer, and did he have a mother complex? The answer to both questions is affirmative, but we should not accept this with negative assumptions. As Carl Jung would later remind us, if we ignore our dreams and repress powerful archetypes, we create problems, not solve them. Don Bosco, in the renewed Constitutions of the Salesians approved by the Apostolic See, is described as 'deeply human, rich in the qualities of his people, open to the realities of this earth; just as deeply the man of God, filled with the gifts of the Holy Spirit and living "as seeing Him who is invisible"' (Salesian Constitutions No. 21). To those towards whom his apostolate was mainly directed – young people in need – Mary the mother figure was psychologically most suited. I venture to suggest that it is also today.

Education should appeal to the whole human being in his or her intuitive, sensible, thinking and feeling dimensions. If we follow the example of Don Bosco's appeal to Mary, we remain true to these dimensions. Furthermore, in an era when a skewed understanding of romantic love as the only vehicle for our need for wholeness has put impossible demands on the relationships between boy and girl, the model of woman which Don Bosco offers to the young in Mary enables them to redirect their spiritual aspirations and unburden the complicated-enough task of ordinary human relationships. Deep friendship and commitment become possible when uncluttered by needs which require an intensity and perfection well beyond adolescent capability.

There are four images of Mary that Don Bosco regularly promoted. They formed a repeated and consistent pattern in Don Bosco's dealings with the young, and they correspond adequately to those four dimensions of human wholeness later identified by Jung (sensing, intuition, feeling and thinking).

The first image is that of the mother: Don Bosco's Madonna. This corresponds to our need for one who is near us, a sensing, present person. A mother's receptiveness is closely connected to the mythical and archetypal 'mother earth', and it is significant in the dreams of Don Bosco that Mary's direction to him was offered in fields and gardens. I find it not at all odd to suggest that the contemporary concern for environment is a good opening for the presentation of Mary as mother. It is a motherhood that has its initial scriptural reference in the primeval garden when the promise is made that the 'seed of the woman . . . will crush the head of the serpent' (Gen. 3:15). The image given us at the end of salvation's history is again the woman, after giving birth in the wilderness 'where God had prepared a place of refuge for her' (Rev. 12:6).

The second favourite image of Mary that Don Bosco promoted was that of Mary ever Virgin. The proclamation of the Dogma of the Immaculate Conception gave him a ready term: Mary Immaculate. There was nothing saccharine in this image for Don Bosco. Rather was it an image of transforming power. As Virgin, Mary was his source of inspiration, his teacher and guide. Here was the intuitive element of the psyche cared for in a dynamic way. Youth needs something to give it greater depth and motivation for existence and Don Bosco offered it through the model of Mary Immaculate.

There is a third image: Mary the beloved of God. Don Bosco's entire life's work was a response to a God who loved and he understood Mary as a model of response to that love. Mary can be a channel for strong human passion and affectivity. There is no doubt that Don Bosco's holiness and work for the young was beyond the accusation of being one-sided and chauvinist, for it involved a tenderness and compassion which gave it wholeness. He did this through a personally appropriated love for Mary.

And finally, there is Mary as the Help of Christians. It is the image Don Bosco is best remembered for. It is under this title, too, that Mary is regarded as Australia's patroness. The Help of Christians certainly has a traditional and historical origin in one or other battle for the Faith, but its finest origin is really the scriptural image of Mary at the foot of the Cross (John 19:25–27), where she becomes the mother of all. In 1869 Don Bosco proposed, in one of his

'Catholic Readings' series, an 'act of entrustment to Mary Help of Christians'. The formula situated the one making the act at the foot of the Cross, alongside John. Don Bosco had a mature sense of Church and Mary's place in it which would be confirmed by the Council a century later.

Mary, as the Help of Christians, was Don Bosco's image for the logic and principle that directed his life. She gave him his mission, and it is the mission which specified the task his followers would have in the Church. He claimed her as 'guide and support'. When finally he wrote a small treatise on the Preventive System, the content of his first dream (youngsters in a field) merged with the form (method – reason, religion, kindness) which was not clear at the time, but which the lady in the dream said, 'would all be made clear'.

The spiritual and educative experience that Don Bosco lived, and that I am depicting as a valid way of encountering young people still, one hundred years later, is one that was explained to Don Bosco by Mary herself, in his dreams. It has the character of a 'Magnificat', a joyful story of the good things God has done for his creatures.

PART TWO

Songs
of
the
spirit

*The heart, gladdened by the realization of a God-with-us,
wants to live in that presence and to help others live so.*

The grace of God, Spirit

If we rejoice in the name 'Christian', then it is helpful to
spell out what that means. It means to have accepted as
true the revelation of God as Father, given to us in the
person and word of Jesus Christ. It means not only to have
heard that this is so and to have accepted it, but also to
have recognized individually one's responsibility to:
proclaim
the love of God, Father,
which comes to us in Jesus Christ, Son,
so that
humankind,
with the grace of God, Spirit,
accepts it,
with a free and firm commitment.
In that list is contained explicitly the core content of the
message that God loves us, reveals that love in Jesus, and
makes it known today through the action of the Spirit.
Implicitly the list contains the elements of an educational
method – to proclaim in such a way that people will accept
freely what they hear, and commit themselves firmly to
doing what has just been done for them.
That '*so that*' is an ambiguous link; the hoped-for result
might occur, but could be obstructed by almost anything
from a school time-table to general human perversity. But
it is the Word of God we are dealing with, a fruitful word
as we are reminded as far back as Isaiah; a word that does
not return empty (Isaiah 55:11). The firm intention of the
proclaiming is to overcome human perversity or whatever
obstacle to achieve the commitment.
Regardless of language, what makes it possible to
approach our Christian mission with such confidence and
finality and strength of intention is the mention of '. . . the
grace of God, Spirit'. The proclamation began with the
coming of the Holy Spirit and it is He who continues to

make it effective in both proclaimers and listeners. In our most difficult moments, this is the line we can recall.

A community of educators might well focus on the implicit educational method. There are many approaches. I have been schooled in the modern proclamative approach of Don Bosco, who offers a way by which any Christian can begin to proclaim Christ effectively to one part of humankind in particular – the young.

To make use of this inspiration, we can note that to catechize is more than to preach or teach religion. To some is given one or both of these tasks; but to all who are baptized is given the task of helping others mature in their faith. What characterizes this task if done in the manner of Don Bosco is the ability to create opportunities for flexibility, for gradualness; the respect for human values; the desire to awaken affection, promote friendship, revive hope, breathe optimism; the sheer urge to attract, gather, and do good for the young.

All of this is available to the baptized Christian in his or her proclamation of the one thing that matters – Jesus Christ. How it is done has much to do with a word whose roots are clear, but whose concept seems a little removed these days. I refer to the word 'spirituality'. It is a word, and a concept, we need to give more time to.

A conviction

I am seized by a conviction that on the face of it is naive. It is the conviction that Jesus of Nazareth is alive and well in our struggling existences, creating the 'new self that has been created in God's way, in the goodness and holiness of the truth'
(Ephesians 4:24)

Is there anything odd about such a conviction? Well, yes! We are pretty much aware of our failures. Who, amongst us, has not made a dismal mess of some situation: a class, a confrontation, a falling-out with someone. We can, and more often than not do, look at our failures. Is it not a scandal that we assert on the one hand that Jesus' Good

News has come as 'power, and as the Holy Spirit, and as utter conviction' amongst us, while on the other hand we can point to the poor response of so many: proposals rejected, an increasing falling-away in faith practice, the expressed opposition to the message of Jesus?

Yes, it is a scandal, but no different from that experienced by two disciples as they left Jerusalem, the whole Jesus-scheme wrecked around them, the victim himself hanging powerless on a cross. What victory could be claimed there? And yet the two on that road were seized with a conviction, finally, because Jesus became present amongst them, and as a result of recognizing him they were challenged to re-appraise his life; what he said, what he did, and how he lived. Once they returned to the practice of Jesus' life, they realized there were not two Jesuses. There was not a risen Jesus and a Jesus of Nazareth. The only Jesus they really knew was the human being they had followed and listened to. He now seized them in faith, and for the first time in the history of the Church we had a spirituality.

A spirituality is nothing more than the personal assimilation of Jesus' life and mission by a follower. Gregory of Nyssa said that the Christian life was a never-ending movement from 'beginnings to beginnings through beginnings' (*On Perfection*). The two disciples were challenged by the risen Lord to see God's breaking in in this very negative way, seemingly, as a new call, a beginning – and we know how this response of theirs was followed by the response of the new community at Pentecost.

For anyone who would educate as a Christian today, the key to effectiveness is personal holiness, a life founded on the life of Jesus of Nazareth. We need to live the Gospel call freshly. How can we live it freshly unless we have read it, heard it, pondered it, allowed it to challenge and change us? Jesus lived, taught, preached in a way that challenged the accepted ways of his society. In the parables, in the sermon on the Mount, there are directives for us as to new ways of daily dealing with others. We cannot afford to ignore them, or reduce them to simply human categories or systems. We cannot.

In the next few chapters I try to tease out this need that we have for personal holiness . . . and not just for ourselves, but so that we may increase the efficacy of our being-with-for.

Lord, give me patience!

I will start with a personal reflection. Real situations spur us on to holiness, not imagined ones. This was end-of-term . . . Enough said?

A sign – one of those posters you can buy at newsagents – was given to me by a group of senior students who know me only too well; it hangs in my room where only I can see it from the desk, because it proclaims brazenly: LORD, GIVE ME PATIENCE – RIGHT BLOODY NOW! Maybe I shouldn't be a hypocrite, and should hang it where everybody can see it. For it tells the story of my life, and probably of my faith. I am impatient because things don't work out the way I had planned. Was it Robbie Burns who said, 'The best-laid schemes o' mice and men gang aft a-gley'?

To put it another way: I am sure the ladies in the office have long ago despaired of the mess on my desk, as mothers reading this may have despaired of the mess in their son's bedroom. And what happens to a nicely time-tabled day? (Schools are meant to be such orderly places.) People don't make appointments these days; they just arrive. Mind you, I prefer it that way. A young person's problems cannot be timetabled. If you choose to live an open door, phone-on-the-hook existence, you choose to live untidily. Nor am I alone in my messy existence. Recent circumstances have brought me into contact with not a few families, and many boys, who can only see crooked lines.

Ah, but remember! Imagine the distracted and distraught tone of conversation between those two disciples trudging their way out of Jerusalem towards Emmaus when the risen Lord met up with them and walked with them. While he walked with them he explained briefly how God was responsible for all those crooked lines in Hebrew history, to the point where a cross and its broken body angled awkwardly into a universe that had killed its saviour. And as the three – Jesus and these two – took the twists and turns of this road to Emmaus, Jesus brought it all together in a wonderful pattern that made their hearts burn within. And they began to live again!

We need this mess to throw us back onto the mercy of God. Life will never be predictable, and God would like us to live in readiness and grateful surprise for his next move. Of course it will mean being tolerant of the unexpected visitor, and being ready to admit once again that we have failed and need God's help. Was the life of those disciples any more tidy, I wonder, after Pentecost? Not really, but it was a very happy and exciting mess they lived in. When the Spirit came down, this was one whirlwind they could be sure God could be found at the centre of.

Make holy the world

For some years now, the historic mansion of the Clarke family at Sunbury has been thrown open to the public for inspection once a year. The fact that this building is now a Salesian school with an intriguing history helps considerably. Young sergeants in the resplendent uniform of the Royal Horse Artillery thoroughly enjoy the task of tour-guide for these occasions, and, as only youthful exuberance can manage, they give a slightly barnacled version of history, involving piranhas in the fish ponds, ghosts in the halls, and ancient paintings on walls.

One painting now hanging in what is traditionally called the King's Room (yes, a future King of England actually stayed there) is of a balding, kindly-faced gentleman, regularly described by the guides as Sir William Clarke, the paterfamilias. I happen to know, however, that it is a picture of St Francis de Sales!

The boys can be forgiven. It is not so common, these days, to find pictures of the saints hanging from our walls. Not that our respect for the saints has changed all that much, but our taste in decoration has. I have recollections from my youth of many saints who ruled from their privileged positions on the walls of various establishments – from the stern, crucifyingly pious to the too-sweet mother-foundresses.

Personal holiness is an essential element in the way of life of an educator. In view of the all-too-common perspective that a saint is someone very different, maybe stern or gentle but certainly other-worldly, it is appropriate to ask: in what do holiness and sanctity consist?

We can fall into the error of allowing a single historical period to colour our opinions and our theology. Our own period is understandably a major influence on us, but it is not the whole story. Holiness and sanctity belong to no specific era but to the entire history of human endeavour under God's grace. While the last few centuries have produced a whole galaxy of saints, the concept belongs as far back as Old Testament times. Certain Old Testament heroes were not known for their moral perfection – Moses, David, Jeremiah, to name but three – yet the Hebrew language unashamedly calls them 'Saints of the Most High' (Daniel 7:18). Essentially, they were called by God.

The New Israel, Christ's followers, came to be known as 'the dedicated ones' (Acts 9:13). Not all would have qualified for haloes, but they acknowledged that, sinners though they were, the grace of Jesus Christ was busy within them, forgiving, strengthening, transforming. Paul had little hesitation in referring to many of his co-workers as being amongst the saints; if you accepted Jesus Christ as your Saviour, then nothing, Paul reminds us in his letter to the Romans, 'can separate us from the love of God made visible in Jesus Christ' (Romans 8:39). The end result was logical for Paul: one's very presence made holy the world.

So many of us can, in some small way, make holy the world around us. We should be convinced that making holy the world is not to be left to a Pope John or a Mother Theresa. We are called to a holiness which is not for our own sake, but to make holy the world – which includes the machine shop and the playground. We may even be sick at home; it matters little. Holiness does not float above the world. We who share Christ's being share in his holiness and are the sacred touch that gets to work on the world wherever we meet it.

The feast of the Transfiguration invites a more scholarly explanation than I can offer, but in simplified terms, I would say that Jesus was teaching the disciples just this message. They might have climbed a mountain to see Jesus

27

in a cloud of holiness, but the crunch came when they had to descend and confront the days ahead. It all comes together nicely in the Lord's Prayer: 'Our Father, who art in heaven, hallowed be thy name'. To hallow is to make holy, and that means to make God present among people. That's why Jesus added immediately, 'thy will be done on earth, as it is in heaven'.

A smile at the right time, quiet attention to the job, vigorous involvement in a game. It can be as much a touch of God's presence in the world as anything.

Prayer

The bit about prayer belonging to one's quality as a human being before one's quality as anything else; about it being what one is rather than what ones does; about it being presence to oneself, then God, then others – that sort of realization seems to touch a nerve. To look at the matter simply, we would want to claim that somehow, as Christian teachers, parents and helpers along the way, we have enabled others to pray and to have an encounter with God. That is not a denominational issue; of itself it has little to do with sacraments, priests, prayers or one or other kind of spirituality. Of itself, I say. Clearly all those other matters can be closely related. But what is this experience of God, this encounter with him?

Of course, I am talking about prayer, but inviting the reader not to jump to the usual conclusions too quickly – for the conclusions are often of this kind:
• I am not very good at prayer myself . . . time . . . knowing how . . . feeling a bit dry.
• It's a bit hard to teach . . . it should be caught from an early age . . . a bit late now to do much about it.
• I haven't had much that I could personally label as encounter with God.
• I'm afraid I'm in the grip of the 'nothing will ever happen' feeling about prayer.

It may all be true, but it should not engender thoughts of

hopelessness about prayer. A few simple things about prayer are very clear to me, and I offer them for consideration.

1 We have a responsibility which we may not shirk to teach others to pray, in particular our young people. We should be seeking to pass on a skill that is authentic – so that it will be recognized as true.

2 Prayer will only ever be true if it begins as inner attention. This presence to oneself can lead to God; it has a very strong scriptual warrant for doing so. But the guarantee that it will do so is on God's side, not ours. Let's not make prayer too much of a mental effort until God gives us the grace to do so willingly.

3 Jesus at prayer was the one going out to meet the One coming to meet him. This is no vague and impersonal image. Jesus named the One as 'Father', and the meeting that the image implies was so vivid for those first followers of Jesus that it directly associated the man Jesus with the God that he named as Father. The New Testament witness to Jesus as divine is more a witness to moments of prayer (Jesus seeking the Father; the Father seeking Jesus) than it is a carefully worded theology. We can learn much about prayer from the New Testament, other than that one chapter containing the 'Our Father'.

There are methods of prayer, of course. But the methods are not the prayer. The way you are is your prayer. Let your method call your attention to that. Set out on an imaginary road, hoping to meet God. You will meet a lot of others along the way. And, I do believe one day you will meet Him coming to you.

Helping the children of God

Do we all have responsibility for the spiritual development of others, or is this responsibility limited to professionals such as the clergy? Is spiritual development distinct from religious education? Is it even a general, non-religious term?

These are real-enough questions for parents and educators who have to contend with world views which separate the spiritual domain from the secular and who may themselves assume such a separation to be the case. I would like to offer the point of view that all parents and educators have a responsibility to help the children of God to develop spiritually.

We all recognize that there is a distinction between what is cognitive, intellectual and rational about faith, and what transcends that. Teachers of religious education know that there is an assessable content, maybe even assessable behaviour, but they also know that religious education in a Catholic school deals with a faith which is a personal knowledge of divine love as disclosed in the life of Jesus. While it corresponds to reason, it is responded to in hope (the possibility of finding meaning) and is lived out in action which, though it begins in oneself, then goes out to others, namely, charity.

It is this faith, hope and charity of the non-assessable kind which forms the content of spiritual development and which all who believe in Jesus are called upon to develop in others. This is what mission is about.

Parents then, will be the prime spiritual directors of their children. The Church is engaged in the task of helping today's parents realize this. Teachers and other adults associated with school (this lets in bursars, office staff and other support persons) come at least second.

If spiritual development is not the same as religious education, then it will happen differently. I would like to put a case for osmosis. Educators who rely on this fail in their task. Knowledge of the cognitive, rational kind does not transfer by osmosis. A teacher with all the degrees in the world will not produce a class of university graduates through simple juxtaposition. But put a person of simple goodness and profound faith in their midst, and something happens. Countless stories in the annals of Christianity testify to that. Faith, hope and charity are transcendent and catching! So, the first task in discharging our responsibility is to be holy, good, faithful and to love God; use whatever synonyms one likes.

The second difference between spiritual development

and religious education is the most important one, but we forget it so easily. Yet what a relief to accept it as true! 'He whose power is at work in us . . .' (Ephesians 3:20). Paul screams it out in his letters. While education undeniably includes the effort of the educand, spiritual development is not essentially dependent on that effort. A better definition of spirituality might be 'what God is doing to us'. Let us freely recognize and give thanks for a Father who calls young people, confirms them in holiness, makes them blameless, perfects them, and for a Son who redeems, directs them to his Father, models life for them and continues to offer fullness of life through the sacraments; and for the Spirit who sanctifies, makes his home in them, gives life, freedom, holiness and personal charisma. Our next task is to actually have that daily-lived awareness that life is grace. If one is Christian and believes in the God Jesus revealed, then one cannot cloud over the recognition of God as giver of life. He does not suddenly cease to give life between the difficult adolescent years of 12 and 19.

I do not remember any specifics of my learning at Year 7 or 8 or 9, but I clearly recall my teachers and many details of their presence to me. Whether they knew it or not, they were my spiritual directors. In fact, from the narrow vision of the child, I suspect that they were seen not simply as part of the Church or of God's people. They were it! They were all God had to offer, along with my family. A sobering thought?

PART THREE

From the heart of a boy

Each piece inspired by, written for, or written by a young person deeply loved in Christ.

Bartimaeus

I suppose it was the Sunday Gospel (Mark 10:46-52) that brought the thought home to me; the sudden realization that the perspective of the Gospel was the reverse of how I had been viewing things. Here was a man, Bartimaeus, who had every mark of the alienated human being, and here was I, thinking of the whole episode in terms of the terrible effect of environment, of culture, society and so forth, on the poor old coot. But of course, the drift of the passage is quite the opposite! 'Go and call him' says Jesus to those standing around. 'Courage', *they* say to him. I had missed all that at first reading. The story – it's more likely to be fact, the scholars say – is not about alienation as a negative effect of society, but about the positive effects of people's faith on someone.

What a lift that has given me, especially when part of a recent afternoon was spent talking to a youngster who might be described as alienated. We were able to look at it from a different perspective. Without this Gospel perspective I know what I would have been doing – thinking of the problem as a set of characteristics like the following:
1 He feels out of place, friendless, restless.
2 He can't find much meaning in it all.
3 He feels powerless and without possibility.
4 He lacks, or has lost, drive.

All true. But where would it have left us? With a set of easily recognizable negatives. Instead, we took a different tack. Not how one feels alienated because of x number of factors, but how Faith can affect those around us. Suddenly, I had a boy who was saying not what others were doing to him, but what he might be able to do for them.

A small victory perhaps. Instead of viewing himself as one being turned away from, he has taken a small step in turning away from his own situation and turning towards a vision of faith.

34

Mark's presentation of the scene with Bartimaeus is obviously a catechetical construction for his own Church. I find that interesting. There was a moment of formal (classroom-like) catechesis in a question-and-answer form. That was conducted by Jesus (Religious Education teacher!). But the more significant part of the catechesis was that conducted by the untrained ones standing around who were prepared to obey Jesus' simple command – 'Go call him, tell him to cheer up'.

The point may now be clear. Every good Christian in his or her next encounter with an obviously 'alienated' character – in the yard or wherever one meets the individual – by his or her own faith view can 'go call him, tell him to cheer up' and do more for the problem than a thousand analyses of a negative kind.

'The Bloke'

Wot's in a name? Wot's in a string o' words?
They scraps in 'ole Verona wiv the'r swords
An' never gives a bloke a stray dog's chance,
And that's Romance.
But when they deal it out wiv bricks an' boots
In Little Lon., they're low degraded broots.

No need to tell you where that comes from. 'The Bloke' was a keen observer of human nature –

Wot's jist plain stoush wiv us,
right 'ere today,
Is 'valler' if yer fur enough away.
(From *The Sentimental Bloke*, by C. J. Dennis)

Ned Kelly, to stay with the Aussie cultural scene, is proof enough of that!

'The Bloke' was more interested in entertainment than moral instruction, but there is something of a challenge in his words nevertheless. We regard the battle of East and West over an 'iota' (the difference between 'homo-ousios' and 'homoi-ousios') with amused detachment, forgetting that lives were lost over such descriptions of the Godhead. Franciscans and Dominicans too, fell out over Jerome's faulty reading of the Greek New Testament . . . and their motives were far more lofty than those of the Montagues and Capulets! The challenge is to look carefully at people, actions, events, and to be critical of the distancing that takes place. The poet in question considered two types of distancing: time, and the dramatic form which elevated larrikinism to love.

I have in mind Chris. Chris had been in a class where C. J. Dennis's poetry was popular. He identified quite easily with the characters and events, and its rough-hewn language, for Chris was a country boy. Chris is now dead, struck down tragically by a rare disease at seventeen years of age. It is true of most deaths of young people that they influence us considerably; this death was no exception. Chris would not have called himself a model student but the facts are that from being a rather wild and unsettled little chap in his first year at College, he had become something of an inspiration to his peers and, in the estimation of his family and teachers, a boy who had begun to show that deeper development of responsibility that a Catholic education purports to invite young people to.

Death is a kind of dramatic form that can elevate a human being's life, a kind of distancing, so I must be careful. But Chris joins that list of young lives that I like to ponder, from time to time, for what it can teach. He was a young person who lived an ordinary life with extraordinary vigour. To be good in the twentieth century is no mean endeavour. It was always so; and Chris was good. Another literary figure, that of Huckleberry Finn, may help elucidate the nature of this goodness. What youth of the twentieth century has not faced Huck's dilemma of what to do 'when it's troublesome to do right and aint no trouble to do wrong, and the wages is just the same?' But Huck's story is an exposure of human failings while retaining an essential faith in human goodness. And at the base of all this, something Mark Twain did not consider, is a faith-inspired sense of responsibility that can make itself felt directly through the grace of God, or indirectly through the moral climate of family and school.

Chris, I am sure, had paid attention to both. He had altered from Tom Sawyer, for whom life was just fun, to a Huck Finn and something better still, for whom life is an adventure, yes, but an adventure that was prepared to meet its moments of seriousness. While Huck had simply to rely on his feeling and experience, devoid of moral guidance, Chris was able to learn to handle life's problems in a moral context that considered morality more than private reaction to private feelings.

The funeral I will always remember for its touching tributes, by his own peers; many tributes. 'He was a good bloke' ceases to be a banal string of words in the mouths of young people for whom Chris was now a never-to-be-forgotten symbol. He was that in life; now he would be that forever.

The life and death of each one of us has its influence on others; if we live, we live for the Lord; if we die, we die for the Lord; so that alive or dead we belong to the Lord.
(Romans 14:7-8)

Godwin

No one could have known, Godwin, least of all you, when we began a new season and a new term, that you would teach us what we struggle to understand: that God can be good when Spring reverts to Winter, life turns to death, and crown becomes cross.

There was nothing more important for us than the fact that you were a fourteen-year-old boy. Especially now, we must resist the temptation to make of you more than you were. Your simple, friendly presence, the fact that you didn't always get 'AA', or understand my writing on the board, is now a precious gift to us. Death has made that so. God, as he has done so often in human affairs, has simply walked into your life and made it clear that your life, and ours, has eternal significance.

This is so, Godwin, because God did the same two thousand years ago. He entered a tomb and simply raised Jesus from the dead. Before that, death was the end, absurd. God cut through that, simply, and it could never be so again. If, in Adam, all had to die, 'now, in Christ, shall all be made alive' (Corinthians 15:22).

Jesus thanked his Father for revealing and making clear these things to mere children. We thank the Father, and we thank you too, Godwin, not only for the gift of your life with all its ambiguities, but also for the gift of your death and the clear knowledge you have given us of God's goodness.

It is banal to assert, along with the poet, 'that the good men do lives after them'. Our faith is greater than that. It is God who has done something good in your life, Godwin. Baptised in Christ you have now died in Christ and come to new life. God has confirmed that in calling you to him. And so, we believe, it will be for us.

On 20 June, I wrote you a small note which wished you a happy birthday. Today, with love, with all my heart, and on behalf of all, I do that once again.

Please pray for us all . . .

Ghost story

Everybody loves a good story, especially a ghost story. Young or old, the human psyche revels in a bit of wildly imagined trauma. Skeletons should not be left to languish in cupboards when they can be made to dance and dangle before the mind's eye!

Morbid, you say? Not at all. I have spent years telling ghost stories and, for nearly two decades, have camped annually with a group of youngsters beside an ancient Tasmanian cemetery. Boys will be boys, and while ghouls amongst the graves are not the stuff of Christian meditation on 'the last things', boys will still be fascinated by those ancient crosses tilting defiantly at time. But what do those crosses mean for them, and can we help them to make some sense of it all? The good old ghost story, I have found, is as successful a way as any into the Christian mystery of life and death.

Do not be surprised, then, at the recommendation to consider the Passion as the 'Greatest Story Ever Told' – as a rollicking good ghost story . . . with a happy ending, of course. When I was just a little tacker we always said: 'In the name of the Father, and of the Son, and of the Holy Ghost'. I must confess that while the loss of bells, Latin, and the prayer to St Michael the Archangel left little impression on me when they fell out of favour, the loss of that sturdy little Anglo-Saxon word 'ghost' – and a holy one at that – did.

With all this in mind, I have encouraged some senior students to take another look at the death of Jesus, to wonder, perhaps, at the many untold stories of those associated with that event. After all some, and it was limited finally to just four of them, decided to select a few details, and tell it the way they saw it or imagined it to be. Wouldn't it be interesting to go back into history and prize open the memories of a few other participants or bystanders, and let them tell it the way they saw it? My brief acquaintance with the classics of Christian spirituality certainly indicates that our great mystics – St Theresa was one of them – have given this type of contemplation a good pedigree.

So, let me treat you to the efforts of one student. Suffice it to say that he is in Year 12 and might one day see himself as a journalist. Now, read on and enjoy the story of Barbara Pilate.

It had been a bad day for Barbara Pilate. Come to think of it, it had been a bad week . . . a bad year. Troubles with the servants (they had been talking of forming a 'union' or some such crazy thing) and troubles with her life. These crazy Jews! she thought desperately. Could it only be a year ago that we were in Rome, amongst civilization . . . friendly people . . . a comfortable villa . . . holiday flat in Frascati . . . a sensible climate! It felt like a lifetime since. And all it had been was one slip – a discrepancy in the accounts – and . . . 'out you go!' said Augustus. Off to this hell-hole. 'Governor of Judaea'. Almost a death sentence, she thought.

These Jews! I just don't understand them, she fretted.

Their weird customs, their tenacity, their resentment against Rome. Always on the brink of a riot or an uprising, it seemed. Who was this latest troublemaker? Jesus of Bethsaida – or was it of Cana? No, of Nazareth, that's it! He was giving her poor husband the jitters. Lose your job as Governor of Judaea, and then what? Britain, Gaul? Ye gods forbid! The poor man, his nerves were going on him. This Jesus was an odd one, actually, she puzzled. She had seen him a week ago, riding into Jerusalem . . . a strangely compelling, even attractive figure . . . still, a troublemaker, and he had to go – her husband was worried grey by him. Oh, those wretched servants! Where are they now?

Weary and dispirited at the end of that day, Mrs Pilate dressed for bed. Her husband was still at the office, pursuing some futile emptiness. Oh help, she thought. We're still going to die out here . . . Slowly she drifted into a restless sleep.

She began to dream. She was drifting . . . floating. Below her, thousands of adoring eyes looked up to her. She felt strangely perfect . . . perfect, and full of an overpowering love for those below, despite the faults she could imagine in their strangely see-through bodies. She could still feel her own flabby body around her, but none of her usual conflict and guilt. She felt . . . whole.

Suddenly, she felt a sense of fear. Nothing had changed, yet she sensed a growing force. Then out of nowhere, huge hands grabbed her. She felt a rush of fear like nothing before. Her hands and feet seemed to burn. She wanted to scream but couldn't. She felt bound, heavy and rigid. Her arms could not move. She realized she was on the edge of a huge precipice. 'Help me!' she cried, 'I'm suffocating'.

She awoke with a bright light shining in her eyes. Her clothes were wet and she felt weak. The light was the sun on her face . . . the sun! Feeling a sudden, confused compulsion she rushed from the bed. Grabbing the nearest servant by the arm she cried, 'Where . . . where is my husband?'

'Off at the palace, ma'am, dealing with that Jesus, I think', replied the startled Jew. She was stunned. 'I knew it', she said. She turned and rushed to her room. A message, she thought. Quickly she scribbled on some papyrus leaves. It read: 'Have nothing to do with that innocent man, because last night in a dream I suffered much on account of him'.

'Here', she screamed to a servant, 'get this to my husband – now!'

What was happening to her? Feelings of guilt and responsibility jammed her mind. She felt agitated and weak. The dream was still so vivid – or was it a dream? Why had she sent that message? Why did she feel sick inside? Where had that Jesus been in her dream?

By the afternoon she could stand it no more. Flinging a large cloak over her head and body, she left by a side entrance, and mingled with the crowd. She walked with extraordinary speed, but without control . . . her soul seemed to direct her. On she went, out of the city, towards Golgotha. She stopped, and looked up. A feeling of horror began to engulf her. There on the hill was a large crowd and three stark crosses. A crucifixion. There was no doubt now.

She soon stood amongst 'the crowd of women who were at a distance'. The dream was directly before her. All the eyes, the faults, the love . . . the figure in agony, on the edge of death for her, for all around her. But they who wept did not understand as she did. She turned away, with all her guilt, her agitation, her fear, washed away . . . taken by perfection. 'If I could just touch his cloak.' It came to her like a tiny flash.

She walked home with a feeling of peace . . . of unending peace in her heart.

Thank you, good scribe, for a ghost story in the good old tradition. But not quite finished, don't you think? Barbara Pilate's story may be at an end. She and Pontius, we suppose, were not sent to Gaul, and we know that he, at least, 'from that day on' became friends with Herod. But then, look at what happened to Herod!

The Passion, as Christians celebrate it, has always invited another chapter. Good ghosts never simply die; they always reappear. 'They were terrified, thinking they had seen a ghost' (Luke 24:37). Good on you, Luke, you wrote a whole new book about that.

In each one, Christ

I

Mid-winter Monday settles down,
The late one scuffs through corridor;

8.55 a.m.
It's June, that out-of-tune
And winter-laden time o' war.
And now a gusty shower wraps
The junk food scraps
Of cellophane about your feet
And peels and bits from empty bin;
The showers beat
On chapel panes and roof of tin;
At classroom doors the first boys
Lounge and hush
And then the bell – all rush.

II

Each weekday reeks with consciousness
Of butt-ends' faint stale smell
From rain-soaked clothes,
Heedless in the grass, grouped,
As boys must be.
With all the other masquerade
That youth enjoys –
One thinks of homework that is done in class,
The stock-in-trade
Of adolescent boys.

III

You turn the pages of his diary,
You thought and wrote, and waited;
You pictured him and saw his face revealing
The thousand pressured moments
Of which his day was formed.
They caught your soul-borne feeling:
And when the page came back

And his self-signed note of lateness stuttered
And his confidence, like a candle, guttered . . .
You had such a vision of the person
As the person does not understand.
You could lean down, Christlike, where
Your face, and his, and Christ's, merged there.
You could write as if your fingers clasped
His shaky, nicotined and conquered hand.

IV

His soul stretched tight across the lives
That people home, and school and street,
Or taut with what I write and say
And what I do, and don't, in heat.
A house that welcomes, school for life?
A parish to evangelize?
A playground – fingers clasping ball,
Assured of friends, and love?
My conscience jerks.

'I am moved by fancies that are curled
Around these images and cling:
The notion of some infinitely gentle
Infinitely suffering thing.'

In each one, Christ.

(With apologies to T. S. Eliot)

This year's answers:
understanding re-enrolment

The economics student who repeated his Year 11 course
noticed that the final exam paper was exactly the same for

both years. He brought this 'discovery' to the attention of the teacher as a matter for concern, to which his teacher replied:

'You are quite wrong about this. Yes, the questions are the same. But remember, this is Economics, and this year's answers are quite different!'

And so it is with re-enrolment. I am addressing this letter to you, because you are the subject of re-enrolment. It may be the first time you have encountered such a process; it may be the fifth time. Either way, you will be wondering what it really is all about. Let me try to explain.

I have said you are the 'subject' – a young person somewhere between the ages of twelve and seventeen. Re-enrolment also has an 'object', which is not, as some might think, merely to write in or erase another name on a computer list. The object is the commitment one makes. Finally, standing between the subject (you) and the object (commitment) is a set of questions, however it is in the nature of those years between twelve and seventeen that the answers will be different from year to year, even though the questions do not change.

Let's establish clearly for ourselves what re-enrolment *is not*. It is not your signature and that of your parents accompanied by a cheque. Nor is it an occasion for pressure to be brought negatively to bear on the partnership that exists between you, the school, your family.

Re-enrolment *is* a rational process by which these partners evaluate and seek to understand better their situation. Given that we all tend to live at some point along the scale between drift and decision, it is an attempt to move away from the former and towards the latter.

Let's be clear, too, that to re-commit oneself for another year does not imply perfection. You would rarely be clear about your commitments, and I do not know a lot of adults who are very clear about theirs, either. Human beings have to live with lots of doubts. That's life. The choice you make is not between simple opposites – to re-enrol or to pull out. In real life, commitment does not mean the absence of doubt or criticism. Once upon a time, I suspect 'commitment' meant simply to obey the rules, but these days we are more careful about our definition. Commitment, as far as we are concerned at the moment, is to have moved towards a statement of intention. That is, to have thought about things to a point where we are ready to act.

As a young person, you are faced with such a bewildering array of choices and opportunity to make comparisons, that certainties are hard to find. Any commitment seems relative . . . it might change. This is why re-enrolment is so important. Properly considered, it actually helps to focus on the one skill that will enable you to avoid the pitfalls; the skill of decision-making.

Re-enrolment, like commitment, is to do with purpose and satisfaction. I would like to suggest that you view the process as follows:

1 Re-enrolment is a valuable exercise if seen in terms of your personal development and your faith development. Commitments are an expression of intention, and they have to be lived out daily and created daily. Each year and each stage brings with it a new understanding and a clearer vision of the original intention. Far from being a threat, re-enrolment is a challenge to understanding. It will not and should not mean the same thing to an intending Year 11 student as it does to an intending Year 8 student.

2 Re-enrolment offers the possibility of involvement of all partners to the Catholic school – parents, families, yourself of course, and even perhaps your parish. The degree of consultation will vary from case to case, but at least these questions should be considered:

a *By the College:* Are you making good use of your opportunities and choosing to be a positive influence? Do your parents show by their active interest that they support the College?

b *By your parents:* Is the College providing the Catholic education they want? Are they able to give the interest that the College demands and meet whatever obligations in justice they should meet?

c *By you yourself:* Are you willing to abide by the rules of the College and enter into its spirit?
Are you prepared to apply yourself to your studies?
Are you prepared to make the College a better place by your positive contribution to all aspects of College life (religious, moral, scholastic, social)?

Are you prepared to be open to the gift of Faith and its development through family, school and church?

3 Re-enrolment involves a commitment to the essential features of a Catholic school, namely, its educational process and the development of the Faith. Especially where your Faith is concerned, I suggest you consider this calmly and without anxiety. Remember, we don't 'have' the Faith, we 'grow into' it; Faith has many stages. Also, commitment and doubt may exist side by side. A critical and searching attitude does not mean loss of Faith. It may mean a certain turning away which leads to a turning towards, e.g. turning away from a child's Faith towards an adult Faith.

You are likely to need help, even with this explanation. Your teachers and I see it as their prime responsibility to help; so do parents. And of course, the matter of re-enrolment should always be the subject of personal prayer. You can be assured of my prayers on your behalf.

PART FOUR

Tierce
de
Picardie

TIERCE DE PICARDIE or **TIERCE PICARDE**. The major chord ending a composition in a minor key. This idiom was common in the sixteenth and seventeenth centuries and the beginning of the eighteenth century.

The obscurity of this musical term belies its significance. The myth of transformation is humanity's most insistent myth. As a final minor chord resolves cleverly into a major in many ancient Church anthems, so do the sorrows of life seek resolution in joy. It was Jesus, raised by the Father, who enabled us to trust this myth forevermore.

Sprung!

We need new words to help us live our holiness. I like 'Sprung!' 'Sprung bad!' the kids say, when caught out. But could we reverse this? 'Sprung good!' I want to try.

The word has a playground vitality – immediacy and a tinge of guilt. Now, the language of spirituality is what has often let it down. We need words that point earthwards as well as heavenwards, and 'sprung' might be a candidate.

Language, of its nature, tends to reduce experience, but it may also enhance it. The great formulas of the Faith with their 'begotten, not made . . .' or 'one person in two natures' naturally reduced an experience that was too hard to put into words. And imagine trying to put the Resurrection into words. He seized them in faith . . . and for the first time the Church had a spirituality.

One Easter, I found myself sitting with a mother and her children on Saturday (Holy Saturday), just hours after their husband/father had died from a painful illness. Trying to understand that experience may help us to appreciate the New Testament experience too.

At first there was nothing but overwhelming shock and loss. Some sleep – drug-induced. Stupid sleep. That was Saturday. Then Sunday, the world awoke, and along with it, those afflicted; empty and with a kind of relief. The relief of no challenge, of no 'suffering with'. The souls of those present were no longer stretching as beings always do in the presence of other beings. At this point the experience could only be described as being like a spring unsprung. Emptiness.

This is the human experience of any bereavement. I owe my understanding here to Sebastian Moore in his fine work *The Fire and the Rose Are One*. But just as I had to turn from this death to the celebration of the Easter Vigil, let us now turn to the Gospel. What if that day after the death of Jesus was the greatest bereavement of all time? What if Jesus had so successfully identified himself with the living God (that's what the Gospels are really on about) that his death, his absence, was the death of the living God? What an emptiness. What despair.

And then it happened. Sprung! Jesus is sprung! And if the word still has overtones of guilt, think of what the empty tomb did to people – quick pay-offs to guilty Roman soldiers, and women running, howling with fear. But, as the Gospel relates it to us, the real fact was the experience of Jesus alive. Souls were sprung. But even more importantly, human beings, whole persons, were sprung. Unnamed associates of the deceased, clearing out as fast as their worried legs would carry them. Sprung! Caught by the no-longer-deceased. Sprung bad! They don't even recognize him. Imagine, the first time the Gospel is preached as a single unit . . . about Jesus of Nazareth . . . proved a prophet . . . killed . . . some women say they saw him – and it is preached as doom, not glory!

But the risen Lord reverses this guilty 'sprung' to a new springing and they bounded back to Jerusalem with Good News and joyous expansiveness.

That to me is 'Sprung bad – sprung good' in action. And, if we believe in the risen Lord, an action repeatable today because Jesus is risen, the springing goes on. The cries of worthlessness and lack of openness to truth are our own cries, and the cries of many people around us. The risen Lord ministers to us in a very human way. He meets us in a ministry of friendship, centres not on our problems but our possibilities, listens to the halting words *about* faith, then responds in a language *of* faith. Finally, he makes sure we have one more basic requirement – a small group amongst whom we can relate our story and express our joy. And once we have cried 'Jesus is risen, Jesus is Lord', our souls are sprung with a conviction, an identity and a mission.

Violence

You can imagine an Australian crucifixion without too much trouble at all: Friday, the Saviour standing on the Hill called Capitol, the proclamation, read rather than written, and the words: 'Well may God save the King of the Jews . . .' Or would it be a scene within the Praetorium, the chamber, and the taunts, the jibes and the jeering, the promise to 'crucify' or make one wear one's words 'like a crown of thorns'?

Some politicians have never minded their language – neither now nor then. But it has struck me so forcibly at the reading of Luke's passion narrative, how Jesus did. He minded it very carefully and under extreme pressure. That assassination, just as political, had this difference, and it makes it worthy of retelling several times in the week that we deem to be Holy.

Holy week leads directly into Easter and a proclamation that has never followed any other assassination: 'He is risen!' We who are Christian could spend time considering why our belief in Jesus crucified and risen can offer us so much hope that what we do in his name will actually be effective.

Re-read the passion narrative as written by Luke. Note the two strands running through it. Violence and evil, even betrayal on the part of those closest to Jesus, and all the while Jesus saying: 'This is my body which is given for you . . .' (Luke 22:19). When insults and physical blows are rained upon him, Jesus' response is: 'it is enough', or 'no more of this' (Luke 22:51). To the really nasty question 'he made no answer' (Matthew 27:14). When Peter denied not once but thrice that he knew the man – a low-down cur, Peter, if ever there was one – Jesus minded his language. A look was sufficient to bring Peter to repentance.

Jesus' language broke the spiral of violence at every

point on his way to death: 'Forgive them Father for they know not what they do' (Luke 23:34). And almost immediately, a sinner who asked for forgiveness received it: 'This day you will be with me in paradise' (Luke 23:43). Lives were touched, not just one but multitudes who 'all went back home, beating their breasts in sorrow' (Luke 23:48). If that is not mass conversion I do not know what is. And what of the centurion who said: 'Certainly he was a good man' (Luke 23:47)? That is a powerful prayer (and prayer is language well-minded in the sight of God) for a converted sinner.

Subsequently, in the writing of Luke, the ones who were more saved (if there can be such a concept) should have been those who were closest to Jesus but who, at his death, seemed furthest away, physically. His disciples, I mean. That offers me a lot of hope as I come to yet another Holy Week and contemplate once more the crucified from the distance of my sinfulness, my distraction, my busy-ness and my badly minded language.

Yes, we who live in a still-violent world are often happy to escalate that violence, all in the name of good teaching ('Listen, son, or I'll . . .'). We may yet contemplate the crucified and learn from him to mind our language in the face of it all; to believe that in this way, and in only this way, will evil be transformed.

Last chapters

Are you one of those who turns to the last chapter of a good book to find out what happens? It is a temptation I certainly find hard to resist. Born of an optimistic father, now a lively octagenarian, and of a mother who some forty years ago entered the glory prepared for her, I like happy endings, live in hope, and revel in resurrections.

But the reality, of course, is often Chapter Twenty . . . halfway or thereabouts through the school year. On the scale of history, it is twenty weeks which can only be re-read, not re-written. To simply quote the final paragraph without recognizing the plot as it now stands would be arrogant and escapist. Prophets, yes, but Peeping Toms, never!

I once thought the British won their wars by writing songs with stirring words like 'Pack up your troubles in your old kit bag and smile, smile, smile'. But they didn't, did they! They won them, if people 'win' wars at all, by stirring deeds. Victory was planted all over rubble, rivers of blood, and in the face of death.

I am sorry if Chapter Twenty seems to harbour sinister elements, but it does, so let us responsibly recognize them and face them:

• Boys, with parental connivance, taking what they can get out of the place and giving little, or nothing, in return.

• Absenteeism: not just one, but many. Not just once, but often. The motives may be good but, as St Paul once said, 'they run well but out of the way', and they certainly make it hard on the faithful ones.

• Lack of full-blooded support for out-of-school activities, especially sports practice.

• Active, visible commitment to Parents and Friends left to the few faithful.

• A scholastic diary can go weeks without a serious effort by those most closely concerned to see that it is viewed, discussed, signed.

Perhaps I do us all a disservice to even hint at the image of war, though God knows even that same Paul, that irritant gnat on the rump of the Roman world, had his 'breastplate of righteousness' and 'sword of the Spirit' (Ephesians 6:14ff). It is not a war, but the mystery of the Gospel I am on about – a Gospel which spoke scathingly of the lukewarm while having compassion for the weak. It is not flesh and blood we are contending with but the mystery of evil which inserts itself into all of our lives, mine as much as yours.

You will need to respect my motives for this to be seen as a positive call to action. My motives are the Gospel which sometimes prompts us to declare things boldly as we ought. It is a call to action to those who could be backing us but are not.

And, of course, there is a final chapter. But did you know that the first written words of the Gospel were the chapters on trial and death? Every Gospel was written backwards, yet look what happened! I believe, I do . . . and I hope.

Have your answer ready

I recall, in university days, reading an open letter to staff and students. It went like this:

> We believe that the Easter vacation serves no useful purpose whatever at present. Coming as it does just a few weeks after Orientation Week, it is hardly the appropriate time for a holiday – after all, that's what it is, isn't it? We believe that an extra week of the summer vacation would receive the wholehearted support of the majority of the University population. What? You actually recognize Easter as a religious festival? You must be joking! Most Christians are four-wheeled. The church can be useful for baptisms, marriages, funerals, and perhaps Christmas, but five days . . . ? Just how many people, now let's be honest, actually believe that Jesus Christ rose from the dead two thousand years ago; and if he did, what does it matter anyhow? After all, that's what we are supposed to be remembering, isn't it? Surely there would be too few believers these days to justify having a five-day holiday. Therefore we propose that the holiday, as presently constituted, be abolished.
>
> *(Signed: Sundry Reactionaries)*

Mind you, there is probably quite a difference between the motivations of 'Sundry Reactionaries' and those reading these lines, but of course, that's not the point of it all . . . The point of it all is 'and if he did, what does it matter anyhow?' We are supposed to be witnesses to a reality that has been transformed by the risen Christ. Ultimately, we do not succeed in this task by simply acknowledging that we are enrolled in the list of those who call themselves Christians, or practising Catholics, even. Someone else – his name was Peter – also wrote an open letter to those who claimed to be so enrolled. He said:

53

Blessed be the God and Father of Our Lord Jesus Christ! By
his great mercy we have been born anew to a living hope
through the Resurrection of Jesus Christ from the dead . . .
Always have your answer ready for people who ask you the
reason for the hope you have.

(1 Peter 1:3; 3:15)

We are being challenged by Easter to renew in ourselves
our awareness of what has happened to reality since God
raised Jesus from the dead.

Well – what has happened to reality since Jesus' resurrection? Do you know the process by which society will
evolve into a more perfect state? I certainly do not. But I
can sense the disappointment at the obvious list of failures
through the past two thousand years by those who have
expressly called themselves Christians and who have hoped
for a more perfect society.

My own conviction is that Jesus' being raised from the
dead by the Father says something about reality as we
know it: God loves, and I can have absolute trust in the
power and goodness of that love. It tells me that the victory
is now. But, you ask, how can one have hope in a world
now transformed when a look around will show just how
untransformed it really is? Aren't you denying reality, the
really real, by asserting this supposed 'new' reality since
the Resurrection? My answer is that it has become painfully
obvious that man alone has not achieved, nor will achieve
much, but that there is clear evidence of the satisfaction of
lives in Christian hope – with the conviction that the
strength and love of God works within them. They do not
give up, they are committed to the world. They work at
their task unceasingly till death. They always have smiles
on their faces. Put simply, Christians who *do* really believe
in the Resurrection don't quit!

Whatever may be our problem at home, in business, at
school – personal problems, group problems – the Gospels
which contain the narrative of the death and rising of Jesus
speak to these problems. And in the midst of every anxiety
and problem, there can be the undeniable conviction: Jesus
lives!

It is good to recall that the followers of Jesus must also
have moved out of the initial clarity that came with the

experience of the risen Lord. As they moved on, after the Ascension and Pentecost into the countryside of the wider Israel, they must have begun to encounter the mystery of their faith. While things were black and white, it was easy. But as the Acts of the Apostles began to unfold in reality, how much grey they must have had to live with.

We all have to live in the 'grey' of life, yet we too are called to say 'Yes' to this mystery. When we gather to seek the reason for the hope that is in us, we do so in the Lord, however, and according to his mind as found in the Gospels. Where we find white in our lives, we rejoice. Where we find black, we beg pardon.

But mostly, we must simply strive to live and create a life of freedom and love where we seek neither to question the motives of others nor to act in a way that our motives will be questioned. In other words, we offer our answer, as Peter goes on to say, 'with respect and courtesy and with a clear conscience' (1 Peter 3:16).

From time to time

Ever had a class of sixty elderly women? 'Beautiful homily, Father', little knowing that you hastily put the words together between getting up late and donning your vestments five minutes later at Villa Maria. I have never felt so hypocritical as at that time in front of sixty faithful ancients, between them totting up some four thousand years of pilgrimage through life.

I tried to suggest to them that Lent is the Church taking its time; that being faithful takes time; that Moses and Elias and Jesus and Jahweh all thought forty days or forty years was not too long to prepare for the final victory . . . and all the while my heart rankled at the thought of the day before. Those bloody kids took twelve hours of my time to put the school mag. together. A whole day gone! 'Beautiful homily, Father'. Codswallop it was, Sister! If I could only believe it myself!

But thanks, Lord. Once again in weakness your power is evident, for the lesson strikes home. Hypocrisy is but another point of conversion, if your grace is present. Dissemblers and pretenders we may be, saying what we are not. But if the last can be first, the foolish wise, the lower can come higher, then what may you be able to make of the hypocrite? I wait in hope.

The lesson that I think I may be learning can apply to others too, if those others are in the helping professions. Lent is a new way of looking at time. If you will excuse an improper regard for etymology, Lent is time borrowed, on loan. People who serve, constantly, as teachers or preachers, tend to take over time and administer it as their own. That, I believe, may be the mistake, and its realization the moment for conversion.

What are the forces that currently influence our use of time? What does time mean for us? What efforts do we make to allow the graceful presence of God to be more apparent in our work and leisure? Check them for yourself, but for me one is the desire to be all things to all; busy-ness as a criterion for personal worth; and the error (maybe) that Lent is just more self-sacrifice in these terms.

And the meaning? Doing things because we either like to or think we have to, but thinking of them as either pointless or compulsive. Doing the school magazine? Going out with someone? Talking to an important caller? The garden? Having a beer? If I like these things, I seek them almost compulsively. If I don't, then they are simply a waste of time! Is there no way out? Ah – the moment of conversion. I can do them all as 'focussed' time; not wasted, not compulsive, but able to find there a God who makes the moment graceful, while inviting me to another time, when it will all make sense.

'Lord, giver of borrowed time, lend me your presence. Take from me the compulsion to save time. Be instead the Saviour who intends the salvation of time . . . for ever and ever. Amen'.

Christ 'unframed'

It can be easy to tame the Cross, confine its effect . . . on a wall or even an episcopal front! It helps to free up 'received' images of the Crucifixion. As for Jesus crucified, so, too, for Jesus risen.

It is the Resurrection which offers hope in nearly everything we are trying to do – which suggests that one can get up in the morning joyfully, despite physical tiredness; that one can face the normal hardships of dealing with people and problems hopefully; that in the midst of sin, depression, brokenness, one can tread with the conviction that all is yet well, because 'He is risen'. That is some claim! It is a claim that is too often 'framed', become tired and untenable because locked away in theological formulation.

Can we be eternally hopeful about situations that appear not to offer any hope? A student who does not seem to want to engage in any conversion, perhaps? Now it is natural that in our human way of thinking, we see conversion as a step-by-step process, the outcome of personal effort, and discipline (self-imposed or otherwise). We also see it as a change of direction, and can find good biblical evidence for that understanding. But then we fail to see a lot of evidence of this happening in our own lives or the lives of those to whom we are dedicated. The Resurrection effects seem a little restricted!

Are we looking at the wrong thing? Stop and view the New Testament evidence once more. Take St Paul. Funny thing, he never describes his own experience on the Damascus road as a conversion. We even note, with interest, that Paul did not change his direction that day. On he went to Damascus – in a different frame of mind, of course, but on he went, just the same. Paul had an instant illumination that brought about a change. No process of reasoning, no gradual moral change. And accompanying it was the imperative to go and do something in the service of the Risen Lord. We are led to recall an event that, in the Gospels, seems to have happened long before the Resurrection but, when you think about it, was written after the Resurrection along with all the Gospels. It was the time when Peter was so overwhelmed by the instant truth of Jesus' goodness that he fell down in front of him, on the shore of the lake where Jesus had borrowed his boat, and said: 'Lord, depart from me a sinner' (Luke 5:8). In the same instance he is both forgiven and charged with a service.

So, instant illumination, revelation, seem to be the way the risen Lord works. Not too much evidence of that today, we say to ourselves . . . again forgetting that there were some three years between Peter's first experience and his finally acting as one who confidently asserted the risen Lord in his life, after Pentecost, and ten years, along with a period of blindness, after the Damascus event before Paul had any real success as a witness to the risen Lord. In the meantime, the old personality, the old instinctive behaviour probably reasserted itself and made Paul a difficult man to deal with; one whom the more conventional disciples admired, but were happy to send away to preach somewhere else.

It is in the light of such reflection that we realize how often we either want too much or too little of the Resurrection in daily events. Too much, in that we look only at the stunning event on the Damascus road and think of it as instant conversion, total change. Too little in that practically speaking, we have discounted there being any chance of divine revelation these days. Wrong on both counts!

Lord, there is a time in my life, surely, for the mystery which is the vision of the Lord on the way to Damascus, and there is a time also in the lives of each of those I love and work for. I ask for the following: The grace to recognize the moments of such revelation as gifts. The grace not to believe that those moments are the whole conversion. And the grace not to take over those moments as "my own", but to continue to leave them open to your goodness, forgiveness, and impulse to serve. Amen.

PART FIVE

Carols and canticles

Paeans of joy, carols, canticles – life has its moments of festivity, its holidays and its holydays.

Cricket and Christmas

Just what would cricket and Christmas have in common? Each appears on our calendars as an end-of-year holiday event; each has its time of waiting and announcement; each has its potential to spark our interest and arouse our feelings; each has become a 'big event' – dazzle, drama and feelings manipulated by media. The two events come along, receive their commercial salute, and pass on into that collection of generally unlived or forgotten rituals that litter our lives.

Cricket and Christmas have something biblical about them. I don't have to argue that case for Christmas, except to lament that Christmas, as it is commercially presented to us, may well be about the absence of God rather than his presence. I understand the Bible to be chiefly a reminder of God's powerful presence. The media can possibly be forgiven for missing the point of it all; things were not much different back in the year One when Jesus came in a small way to little people, in an insignificant corner of the world. The local political campaign had gained all the limelight, and the 'stars' of the show were too bright for all but three to notice another star illuminating the centre-stage.

Does cricket have biblical origins? I doubt it, though some devotees refer to Wisden's Almanac as the 'Bible' of cricket. I would also have to say that, like the old soldier who used his pack of cards to remind him of the truths of Christianity, the battle for The Ashes could be a salutary reminder of Christian belief in the death and Resurrection of the Lord. Cricket, after all, is a game where hope rarely dies: down but not out, struck but not bowled, attacked from all sides but not caught out . . . and all in the hope of a 'gerlorious resurrection' as Lawson (the real Henry!) might say. You don't have to alter the language much to accommodate that of Paul, that lively captain of the Corinthians,

60

who also considered our life in Christ as 'this treasure in (an) earthenware vase' (Corinthians 4:7). Shades of the ashes and the urn!

But I had better not stray too far down this path for fear it may test the patience of the most tolerant Scripture scholar. There is another game which leads to the heart both of The Book and The Game. If the chief message of the Bible is to bring to us God's presence, then cricket has three of the virtues by which a young person may learn to become whole, and through which God's grace may find entrance, at least to the back-room of one's being where the real work of living and growing takes place. It is here that God is at his most pervasive. While the virtues are not the classical three – faith, hope and charity – you will recognize them nonetheless.

The first virtue is that of **manners**. Manners give to the careless acts of every day an aspect of ceremony, and they enhance the more considered acts. How to behave, and what is expected, this is the substance of manners. Cricket always used to espouse this wonderful quality. What a pity it would be if the over-intrusive media made it necessary for a captain to ask permission of the camera-man for a break in play rather than his peer out on the field. How close we are to losing the real meaning of the phrase 'it's just not cricket' when we see some of the examples of 'yobbo' behaviour out on the pitch. Real cricketers have manners. Captains are captains to be obeyed, just like dads should be dads who earn our respect, and prime ministers should be able to rule fair-dinkum citizens rather than a bunch of cynics. God is to be knelt to in awe and worship – at his behest, not according to our whim. Manners don't destroy feelings; they allow feelings to be channelled, understood and received.

They help us not to abandon small moments to the smothering mass of democratic fellow-feeling. Manners allow God's grace a regular opportunity to take account both of our positive and negative feelings. When God gave the world Jesus in the way he did, it was a gracious, mannerly act on his part; an event that was not even allowed to disturb the process of politics or people at the time. The description of the birth, and the subsequent visit by the Magi is one which demonstrates all the wonder of gentle, mannerly respect and behaviour.

Yet another virtue of cricket is that of **style**. Hard to describe, exactly, but easy to recognize. Perhaps it is the happy union of individual feelings adjusted to external expectations. Style can be there in the carefully flighted off-spinner, the almost imperceptible contact between bat and ball that sends it crashing to the fence past gully. Style is not so obvious in the outrageous bouncer, or the last-ditch walloping six from a desperate tail-ender. It seems to me that Jesus came in style to people, despite what appearances might say. It is not pomp, but the right feeling for the right moment. The sacraments properly lived are but Jesus' style, the now consciously lived rituals of the Church's life. If we know what style is, we can live out Jesus' becoming flesh many times a day. Can we make our family moments sacramental as God seeks once again through us the right moment to come into our midst?

And finally, there is the sense of **timing**. It is the virtue of tact. To everything there is a season. Time has a quality. Moments have sizes. All batsmen know that. There is a time to stay there and just block; there is a time to get on with the game. God had great respect for time. I cannot believe that the first Christmas happened when and where it did in a divinely arbitrary manner. There was a time and a place for God to become man. God's grace has a quality of tact about it. I could not believe that his grace is digital, detached from its context. The parable which tells of the eleventh hour payment was a reminder of God's timing rather than ours, and the fact that time does not just march logically onwards. Don't we so often recognize this with our calendars, which we adorn with beautiful pictures to show that other side of time that cannot be measured. Tact might seem to be a lost art. We will have to learn again to feel time.

Yes, cricket and Christmas do have something in common. If we attend to the real meaning of their ritual and their quality as events in our lives, we may yet be rescued from the squads of emotion or the mass of imprecise feelings that come our way on an afternoon in Bay 13 (well

62

known to Melbourne cricket and football lovers) on Boxing Day.

The light of Christ

'What you can't see won't hurt you' is the kind of epigram which mothers mumble over the cauldron as yesterday's left-overs go into today's stew. It is an understandable attitude for economy-conscious cooks (or so mothers think) except that it fails miserably as a moral principle when one is caught contemplating Rover's bones for the soup stock. Yes, it did happen, and I am still here to tell the tale. But the dictum would appear to operate quite generally as a moral principle, and with far more serious consequences than was the case with Rover's bones. For most of us, the principle had to apply for Halley's comet. Despite an intense media hype, the naked eye, mine at least, suffered both strain and delusion in its efforts to fasten onto this scattered mountain of primordial debris. It has now passed on without significant impact on my life. I console myself that the longevity which runs in our family may provide another opportunity in the year 2061!

There is another star which has not hurtled off into the cosmos. It did, in fact, once graciously hover to dwell amongst us. That moment is celebrated annually yet, alas, it is a celebration that has become less and less visible in its original brightness, unseen through the dazzle and flash of tinsel and foil. Jesus is our Saviour and the light of the world. The one thing he did ask of us was to be acknowledged. If we cannot 'see' him for other 'lights' will that hurt us? Jesus unseen is Jesus unacknowledged. Jesus unacknowledged leaves us in our sins.

Young hearts beat high with expectation at this time of the year. It is a mood we should not ignore, though in itself it has little to do with either the First or the Second coming. Excited expectation and hope for the future are too precious elements, located deep in the human consciousness which are too precious to be allowed to be trawled by television alone, and for commercial purposes only. Families and educators (and families are the first educators) can find, beneath the legend and romance surrounding Christmas, some weighty truths for twentieth century mortals. Here are some suggestions.

Being at home for others

The story of Jesus' birth teaches us an interesting lesson about hospitality. The cave or stable was 'home', and anyone was welcome. Shepherds and kings came and went on their own terms. Jesus, Mary and Joseph had created a free space where no one need be afraid and where the visitors could be human in their own personal sort of way. The Gospel story further fills out such allusions. Jesus felt 'at home' with Martha, Mary and Lazarus. Jesus was made to feel 'at home' with Zaccheus. More and more today, the problem we experience is that of making our house a home. We will be told each Christmas that a video, or microwave, or swimming-pool will do just that. But, we recall, home is a free space where people can be human in their own way rather than desperately cling to others, or immerse themselves in possessions. Does our home provide time and space for its members to understand themselves and listen to others? Someone who is filled with ideas, opinions and convictions cannot be a good host. There is no inner space to listen; no knowing the gift of the other.

Bethlehem is not Disneyland

The transference from screen to real life is an easy one. We live in that kind of belief, we educate to mastery, and we even press Christ at times into the service of a Church which we fondly hope will be a powerful force in the world. We have got it all wrong, of course. That babe was powerless. He claimed eventually to be 'The Way' not to be 'The Greatest'. Maybe this truth can help us come to terms with our feelings of helplessness while the world goes mad around us. What is going on in the world is often going on in your heart and mine. A humble confession of our part in the human condition might be the most freeing experience of our lives! I have sometimes asked a distressed and wronged individual to just admit his part in the human condition of sinfulness and to forget being wronged for the moment. It is a new perspective on hurt – and it is what Christ did. He did not cling to his superior equality with God but humbled himself to become man, yes, even to be wronged and put to death. This way, hurt ceases to be a painful interruption to our plans, and becomes instead a chance for conversion of our self and others. It becomes the opportunity for compassion rather than for anger.

Christmas is for celebration
Look! The world is good and holidays are happy times. Christmas is for celebration. As Gerard Manley Hopkins once put it: 'The world is charged with the grandeur of God. It will flame out like shining from shook foil'. Let Christ emerge from the mass of undifferentiated feelings, and appear as evidently alive in our world. May we believe this as the world gears up for Christmas. God is good.

The Pope and the C.I.A.

I should own up immediately. What follows has nothing to do with the Pope or the C.I.A. I have only used that headline to entice you into reading this chapter. No one, except the cigarette companies, has yet been forced by law to point out the hazards of mistaking a book by its cover. I am no lawyer, but 'caveat emptor' is still, I suspect, a valid legal principle. My excuse for an arresting but misleading title! Curiosity always wins out, doesn't it, as I found out recently in a bookshop. I am an inveterate browser, and *A New Sister for Julian* was a title that naturally caught my eye, not that I am unhappy with the one I already have. It turned out to be a well-illustrated booklet on pregnancy and childbirth. I am sure onlookers were amused. I felt, in Roman collar and all, as embarrassed as a Bishop in a bra bar!

Holidays, my friends. That is the real topic. We might well take up the Pope on another occasion. Holidays are upon us again – for the first, or second or the next time in an unending series of holidays, depending on your world-view. While mums fret and dads just get on with it, and the kids enjoy at least the first three days, a very precious event is given to us to make something of. By the grace of God and the Government Gazette, a set number of days are offered. We will leave Government out of it; even my potplants wilt these days when the Treasurer appears on the screen. But I am deeply interested in the grace of God. God only knows if the Pope has a link with the C.I.A., but it would be a pity if only God knows of the link between holidays and his grace.

My thoughts, at this point, are not original. I picked them up while browsing, once again. The title was odd enough to attract one's attention immediately: 'An Offering of Uncles', by an Anglican priest, Fr Capon. He wasn't on about holidays at all, but I am sure he would approve of the application. Fr Capon makes a plea that we rescue three words: *place*, *time*, *history*. Let me explain as I understand it.

We like to believe that we see ourselves living in places, acting in time, the protagonists of real history. But as with so many other things, are we dealing only with substitutes, and misleading ones at that? Think of a boy on holidays, down at the local creek. Now, that is a place – its rocks, slippery banks, its mud. For a small boy, this is as good as the Garden of Eden, with all its temptations. But what are the adults doing, meanwhile? Seeing it as a space, rather than a place, something appearing on the shire map as a space to build a bridge or a bike-path over, to seal forever in cement.

So for time. Have you bought him a digital watch? It will certainly answer the question 'What is the time?' But it won't answer the question 'What is time for?' and I suspect that that is the more important question. We are fooled by the universally valid (or so it seems) belief that 'time' is sixty seconds per minute, and is one of the few things to outlast the onslaught of metrication. But again, ask a boy on holidays what is the time, and he just might tell you that it is time for going fishing, or playing a game with his mates. Can you measure that? Can you measure an un-seasonally spring day in the middle of the winter term? I can assure you that 'recess' in the middle of the school day has immeasurable value, and the hint of eternity shines through every game of handball. What, then, of glorious holiday moments?

Any theoretician will tell you that the co-ordinates of time and place make history. And well they might, but their substitutes will at best make 'chronicle', never 'history'. If a youngster says holidays are boring, then he or she has simply chronicled the day: got up at 8.05, went for a walk at 10.15, watched telly at 5.45 . . . Going for a walk at 10.15 could be a simple alternative to looking after a dreadful little sister, or it could be the chance of a lifetime, a high time of distraction and real interest. History cares which. Chronicle does not.

We all like to think that history exists. No doubt we all act as if it does. But are we sufficiently obsessed with every thing, every person, every real place, every real moment of time, the mysterious conjunction of which is our history? It is no indecent obsession. My fleeting encounter with *A New Sister for Julian* raised a number of questions in my mind: why did man invent marriage beyond sex? Why are adolescents often more interested in the latter than the former? It could be that sex is seen as simply a moment without shape, or direction, or gist, or particularity. Maybe it needs marriage to make history. Two lives in mysterious conjunction. Two histories deliberately criss-crossed. Have the adults in the lives of the adolescents taught them that yet – given them that example?

I appear to have strayed from the topic. Really I haven't. Holidays are a grace of God to be used, to make history. It will need real people – adults, youngsters – to make that. God forbid that holidays should ever be the occasion for falling from God's grace. Other than all the classic ways of doing that, a 'boring' holiday would be that, in my estimation. If you are home, then home is a place, not just a space. If it is 12 o'clock then it is time for something, not just an empty digital dot on the day.

God – the one that Jesus revealed – had his act together, somehow. The writers of Old and New Testaments are often chastised for writing poor chronicle. Getting the creation of the world into seven days was more a human feat than a divine one! And the Gospel writers, if harmonized, have Jesus moving around Palestine faster than today's Israel can invade Lebanon. No, God made history, and desired to become part of man's history. He cared for a place and a time and gave it Jesus. Jesus made sure that all place and all time would henceforth and heretofore become history – through him, with him and in him.

There is, truly, a hint of holy in holidays.

Of men and mountains

Great things are done when men and mountains meet.
This is not done by jostling in the street.

(William Blake)

'And what did you do during the holidays?' One may well ask or be asked the question many times on return to school or normal duties. I would like to share an experience and some of the thoughts it provoked, having spent some time in the high country. It is exciting to traverse the high country; to find and follow a track through dense forest, or across windswept treeless ridges, down deep wild valleys and over high mountains. Or it can be even more challenging still, with no known track, to plot one's own course by compass and map.

You have heard of Calvary? Popocatepetl? Carmel? Sounds like an exercise in trivial pursuit. Not hard to guess what they have in common (besides the letter 'C'!). Each has invited an ascent of one kind or another, none of which has been trivial. Our own Australian Mt Kosciusko seems to slip easily into that mouthful, but climbed from the Geehi, via Hannel's spur (the way Strzelecki himself did it), ease is quickly vanquished by one's years, heat, haze, and March flies. Human diminishment is a poor match for this kind of mountain, but we made it!

There are easier pursuits, and it is about one of these, Mt Howitt, that I now write. It is a mountain accessible either to the walker or the four-wheel driver, though it would be true to say that a certain tension exists between

68

these two categories. Fortunately they approach the mountain from opposite sides.

Now there are huts 'in them thar hills', not always to be relied upon, I might add. Some are in sad disrepair, some are private and locked; almost all share with the local bush rodent. 'Ratty' is a clean-cut version of his more repulsive city cousin, is somewhat unassuming, and does not care to distinguish much between soap and cheese. In addition, he is happy to enter your pack by the most direct route. We chose to use our tents.

Mountains inspire the writer and, I imagine, would inspire anyone who has tried to put pen to paper. Proof of this are the interesting log-books to be found in these huts or under cairns. Most entries are reflective – penned by those gripped by the mana of the mountains. Some seek, like the ancient Shamans of Siberia, to communicate to ordinary mortals truths learned only through solitude. Some are downright frank and not a little rude about the difficulties and hazards faced. Since the students of Timbertop regularly clamber about these particular mountains, one can follow a more or less continuous series of reflections by young people, of astonishing depth and frankness. Why, somewhere on these sodden pages, the future King of England has reflected on the realm laid out before him. It is a realm which he would realize has no single monarch, for it is co-governed by all who have written there.

To those whose health and circumstances allow the opportunity to visit such a realm, there are many discoveries offered. It is a realm which has one character in the high country, another on the promontories and coasts, and yet another deep in the gorges of the nation. I have found, and continue to find, the outer landscape of the Australian bush an invitation to explore the inner landscape of the soul, what Morton Kelsey has described as 'the other side of silence'. There is a link between both explorations, the former leading easily into the latter.

Despite an International Year for Youth, and several Years of one character or another, people still ask 'what's wrong with the world? Kids? The lot?' It is the wrong question, really. Each could be asking the question 'What's wrong with me?' The quiet or the roar, the height or the depth of the Australian landscape can lead one to both questions and answer. Each one, after all, has an undreamed-of potential, and has often failed to be aroused into the sheer vitality of 'I'.

Is it any wonder the message of Jesus is so carefully presented, by a Matthew or a Luke, in a particular geographical setting? Ultimately it matters not whether Jesus sermonized from a mountain or a plain, but that he spoke where people could be induced to listen, could be aroused and lured by him into the discovery of their landscape, his Kingdom, within. 'The Kingdom is very close to you', said Jesus (Matt. 4:17). 'Seek it' (Matt. 6:33). I note that his instruction to us was to seek. The finding should follow. Resurrection followed Calvary, transfiguration followed Tabor. I have learned from my mountains that seeking does have its rewards. Finding is God's part of the deal.

We have set up sacred places which we visit. They often contain little surprise for us. The greatest surprise is to find the sacred in the commonplace and perhaps even in the profane. If God has revealed himself in the breaking of bread, then there is not so much need for miracles any more, do you think? I must say I have enjoyed the unaccustomed space of the bush, the surprises of nature, and the inward journeys begun, but not yet finished. The experience, far from being an escape, has taught me to come back to things that are just as important, to centre down, to dwell within. Somehow the office or the classroom won't be so cramped again, and the everyday will be more important. While it has been good to have been clambering about the roof of the country, it will be just as good going about each day's adventure back home. We are close to God (or He to us) – closer than we think. The Kingdom is within. We may determine to enjoy the 'Little Way' of trivial pursuits in between the impulses of more challenging ascents.

Praise the Lord for the long weekend!

Australians love the 'longweegend'! The concept inspired one Australian social psychologist to explore our national character under the title: 'The Land of the Long Weekend'. However, it happens that we so often celebrate our long weekends with not a little cynicism and restless superficiality, since they are occasioned by commemorations of national importance. Despite the most moving speeches by civic or clerical leaders, the younger generation seems quite unmoved.

As Christian educators, we are faced with an interesting challenge. The challenge is to offer such meaning to life that there will be purpose to celebration. The 'feast-day' has always been an important element of the Church's pedagogy. There are feast-days of obligation, and there are optional feast-days. I firmly believe that unless we make good pedagogical use of the latter, the former will be seen simply in terms of their imposition. Schools and families have the opportunity to declare a feast-day for themselves – not holy days by precept, not an 'ought', but a freely selected 'could'; a possibility, a chance to do something especially joyful and creative.

Let me use a working definition of the feast-day – a space set aside within the rhythm of daily life for celebrating meaning in our lives. It is also a space for educating and evangelizing in the Catholic community. The feast-day is an opportunity to demonstrate that life has a meaning and that it goes somewhere – because if not, then to celebrate such a day joyfully would be an outright cosmic lie, a charade. Just as a mother's reassuring 'She'll be right' to a child asserts a deep belief in the rightness and orderedness of the universe, so does a well celebrated feast-day, because here we set out to celebrate the positive in life.

Take, for example, a feast-day which celebrates the existence of the group, say the school. We need to be clear in our minds about the values this day will celebrate. A feast-day without values loses itself. I suggest we present the day as a memory: a memory of a gift. Everything we have at the school is a gift of those who set up the school, worked in it, built it up, handed it on to us. On the other hand, we can also present the day as looking to the future, because we now have a task – that of handing on the school and all it stands for, to others. The values of the day, then, are a sense of thanks and a sense of duty.

It was the young Saint Dominic Savio, pupil of St John Bosco, who would say to a newcomer at the school: 'Here holiness consists in happiness'. There is something about youthful joy which is very wholesome, and a feast-day, particularly one given religious significance, can easily link wholesomeness with holiness. Of course, there will be forces working against us – the restless banality and superficiality, and centrifugal elements of individuals with a private rather than a communal sense, or who have little meaning in their lives to celebrate. These will fail to see values in gratitude, involvement and future task. But we must not let such forces dictate terms to us. Let the feast-day be a happy day with liturgy, eats, games.

With experiences of this kind, we can view the famous long weekend with a little more serenity, and indeed consider it for its possibilities, for it offers us the basic step towards a feast-day – a space set aside within the rhythm of daily life. If we have demonstrated that such spaces can be celebrations of the positive, in fact a celebration of centring on values, then it is possible we have offered a new twist to days that might otherwise be simply a scramble to country or coast. For the truth is that we are seeking outer space from the city in order to find inner space where the soul can settle in truth.

Australians may yet learn to praise the Lord for the long weekend.

Smile! God loves you!

A schoolyard never ceases to fascinate me, and never more so than on the first day back at school. Hundreds of moving bodies. Hundreds of interesting histories criss-crossing in a universe of youthful exuberance. How easily we assume that most of these histories are strangers to one another. Not so! Look at it from this point of view. Human beings are really very self-aware creatures. Even alone in a crowd one of us is in continual dialogue with himself or herself. By just being us, we are dramatising our existence to one another. Every moment, even standing still, is a way of saying 'This is me'.

Does it strike you just as strongly as it strikes me, then, that the only strangers in that schoolyard are the ones who have deliberately jammed the messages that their being sends out, or who themselves deliberately ignore the messages they receive?

Human beings are communicators first, and by nature; they are strangers second, and by deliberate choice. That kind of shakes you up a bit when you fully realize it. May each moment be for us a moment when we seek to build upon our God-given desire to be in front of another, which is another way of saying that we really believe we are important enough to be recognized by the other. And may each moment also be a moment for recognizing the other as important, simply because the other is experiencing what we are experiencing. May we be tempted to ask why this is so, and may we be open to the possibility that it is so because God made us for the same reason . . . He thought He was important, and wanted to address that to someone. And on it went . . .!

May none of us be strangers to one another. May we seek to remove any jamming from ourselves or others that gives rise to the word 'stranger'. There is much talk of peace in our world. The gathering of a group of total strangers in the ancient city of Assisi by Pope John Paul II in 1986 was one of the most startling actions for peace the world has seen. Peace, in this gathering, emanated from a simple premiss: the simple openness of the spirit of St Francis who was stranger to no being. Every being, even animal beings, can lead to contemplation of our importance to one another because we are important in the eyes of God.

Smile! God loves you!

PART SIX

Raise me a chorus

A chorus is sung by many at once. There is an art in 'raising a chorus'! There is an art in raising a youngster! Family, school, parish and the youngster are the four 'parts' that come together in the great chorus of Christian education. Here, finally, we come to terms with the pastoral educative project.

Re-equipping each other

Catholic education is a sensitive and delicate issue. I became painfully aware of this during a homily when a gentleman walked out at the mention of what is, after all, a classic line from Church teaching on Catholic education: parents are primarily responsible for the education in faith of their children. Why should there be such an anxious reaction to this suggestion?

The anxiety, I believe, stems from the feeling that maybe Catholic schools, faced with an apparent failure to transmit 'The Faith', as it is traditionally understood, are now attempting to put the blame at the feet of parents, and parish, for that matter. It is an understandable anxiety, but surely far from the truth. What, then, is the problem? And what should our approach be?

In rather simple terms, the problem seems to be this: not so many years ago, the Catholic school educated youngsters for the Catholic Church – everything followed from the duty felt by Catholics to send their children to a Catholic school: religious instruction in the first place, and religious practice to follow. In a world which had a known order, and where the Catholic knew precisely where he or she stood, that seemed a straight forward task, and parents, parish and school each knew their part in the process.

But is that the case today? To regard school as a place for moulding the young and fitting them for society (the existing order) is to ask the impossible – and this is as much so for 'Catholic' society in general, because the distinction has become so blurred these days. What is the existing order? What will it be in ten years time? Schools of course have not remained static over the years. In fact there have been considerable developments both in rationale (the 'why' of education) and practice. Witness the much more person-centred processes, the attention given to stimulation of critical and creative thought and action, and the almost overnight technological transformation through the introduction of computers. Schools are not at fault in taking and exploring these paths, but they are tending to grow further away from the family and other institutions (such as the parish) which may not be developing at the same pace or in the same way. Result? Misunderstanding. All of this affects education in the faith.

If that is the problem, what is the solution? Brave person, he who attempts to offer a simple solution! The Catholic school, of course, must continue to educate in a context inspired by Gospel values. As a believing community the Catholic school must attend to its duties – it can only be a believing community if it comprises believers. And the Catholic school must formally educate in the Faith, transmit knowledge, inculcate attitudes, demand certain behaviours. But, and perhaps more importantly, all partners in the task must find new ways of working together. The old partnership is to be re-established where it has broken down, but it is hardly likely to be the same partnership, since things have changed. For a start, there are four, not three partners – parent, parish, school and student. The student can no longer be regarded as the object of education. He or she is the protagonist in a process which will continue well beyond formal schooling.

Successful religious education ceases to be the result merely of good teachers in the classroom. The real question of faith must be posed in other places too – in the courtyards, the parish centres and the homes. We must find ways to merge those spaces and those who people them into an *educative community*. Herein lies the task of re-equipping each other for the delicate task of Catholic education.

I have been raised and trained in a philosophy and practice of education which has elaborated the concept of 'The Educative Project'. The final chapters of this book present such a project inasmuch as it applies to the school, but I would want to make it clear that the school is only one setting for such a project (albeit a privileged one). Any community, starting from the family, which involves young people, is capable of elaborating for itself an educational project, which I would define as a concrete plan meant for a real space and time, which puts the principles of growth (personal and faith) into action.

From all that has been written in the previous pages, I would like to draw out a little more schematically the basic elements of an educative project inspired by the life and ideals of Don Bosco. Clearly, at the centre of the project is The Person, seen holistically. To deal with the young you have to be something of a psychologist, sociologist, philosopher and theologian all in one. While that sounds demanding, it would be disastrous to shrug aside the effort required to accompany the growth of the human person.

There is a style which distinguishes Don Bosco's project. To begin with it is pastoral (see Part One of this book). It proceeds by way of proposal, especially the proposal of positive experiences of whatever kind, to the extent that, swamped by positive offers, the youngster is less inclined towards acceptance of destructive offers that abound in our society. This is a 'preventive' approach in the original sense of that word – getting in first! The educator also aims to set up an environment characterized by at least the following elements: family spirit, climate of festivity, invitation to creativity, reasonableness and flexibility, insistence on daily duty, real effort and involvement of the young persons themselves. This is carried out in the triad of Reason–Religion–Lovingkindness which can only work on a personal basis if the educator is prepared to be present, right in there among the young.

Finally, there are specific areas that such a project must cover. Since it is the complete human and Christian development of an individual we are dealing with, such a project is preoccupied with the education of a person in his or her actual context. Above all, it seeks to relate the faith dimension to life, so the project is of its very nature a form of evangelization and catechesis. The entire activity takes account of the need for the individual to belong to and contribute to a community, which in the real world implies selecting a 'calling' in life and the ability to work within one or more of the groups that make up society.

The way things are

You can spare yourself the trouble of being all things to all people, of debate, wide reading, discussion, raising important questions about life, but only at the cost of boredom and a kind of fatalism about the world around you. When reality means simply to be immersed or submerged in a sea of information, without form, without question, then we become passive, shiftless, bored, even anxious. In this mode we can neither understand the present nor plan for the future.

It is crucial to be a learner in an era that swamps us with data. But how? How do we organize our learning and our teaching, for information is not self-digesting? It might seem that teachers and students have enough to do fiddling with the mysteries of chemistry, computers or Chaucerian English, but the real challenge is critical learning; to have teachers and students who, while attentive to the detail, are prepared to pose questions and point out hazards.

Enter the Gospel. And at this point, as a minister of the Gospel, I repeat on its behalf an immense claim. Jesus turns reality upside down; stands it on its head; observes, pokes, probes and ponders and then says: 'Now you can see the way things are'. He is a model of critical learning.

Take that part where he comes out with his own strong reservations about human teachers. 'Call no man teacher' (Matthew 23:10) he says. Was he just being trendy, subversive? Because in reality Jews respect and prize their teachers. It is interesting that Jesus would have observed the rabbis cultivating status, and in the very presence of these professional 'knowers' he advised the learners to respect the hiddenness of God, the very core of things. The effect of such interventions was that Jesus' listeners saw him as one with authority; somebody wildly new in the tired old world of Jewish religious discipline.

'A man went out to sow . . .' (Luke 8:5). Here is Jesus at work again, probing and questioning. In reality, this passage is not about a sower, nor a harvest. It is about what happens to individual seeds – they move naturally to fruitfulness, thirty fold, sixty fold, hundred fold. The farmer can expect such results if the conditions are right. Jesus is asserting: 'You can confidently know that this is the way things are'. But he goes further – 'So it is with the hidden goodness of God within you'. If you are open to this you will be fruitful! Now just let this constant claim of the Gospel offer its criticism to our educational system and what do you have? A powerful warning to be wary of a system that is prepared to label you as a success or failure without reference to the hidden goodness of God within you.

What Jesus gave to his contemporaries, and what he offers to us, is the challenge to think prayerfully, which also means to think critically, but in a way that is grounded in the mystery of being where God is good. Jesus would want to tell the parents, teachers and students of today that it is not enough for the laboratory to initiate the young learner into the mysteries of science, or for the debate to exercise the speaker in the skills of argument, or for the orchestra to produce the correct series of tones. Each of these discoveries must teach the learner that he has only a small grasp on a truth which he recognizes as greater and greater. It must teach him to respect the core of things – the hidden goodness of God. It must give him confidence that things are good because God is good. This is the Preventive System in action. Jesus could die on a cross powerless, at the mercy of the evil in the world. He could even probe the very motives of the Father: 'My God, my God, why have you forsaken me?' (Matthew 29:46). But he could still be virtuous, feel virtuous, simply because he had grounded his whole existence on the belief that God is good.

Have we met this challenge? Is our Catholic education teaching young people to think prayerfully? To be critical of society in a good and helpful way? To feel virtuous simply because they are good, rather than because they have power, or friends? To feel virtuous especially when unemployed, or even when feeling the absence of God, simply because they have been taught to respect the hiddenness of God? I would not know the answer, except that I feel good whenever we gather at the Eucharist and thank God for his goodness to us, or when on some occasion we gather to recognize the gifts that young people have to offer in excellence and effort.

Education is personal

Since we live in a world where technological advancement is taken for granted, it is logical to imagine a classroom where the exchange of words and ideas takes place purely by electronic means. It is possible but not desirable; we would not want it to be so, and why not? Because we have this feeling that to know is a personal act, and that knowing as in either learning or teaching requires personal relationships.

Television has given birth to marvellous historical productions. Such productions are based on this feeling. Any year 8 student can study the facts about the Anzacs, but embody those facts in a story that features Paul Hogan playing himself, and your year 8 student now believes he knows about the Anzacs. I do not want to enter into debate about the factual adequacy of television history. I just want to recognize that words cut off from persons, or the history of a people frozen into abstractions, are only half knowledge. All words are spoken by a human voice, and we should not treat ideas firstly as abstractions, but rather as human sounds. Our first question should not be 'How logical is that?' but 'Whose voice is behind it?' Not 'What song is that?' but 'Who is the singer?'

How easily we can forget this when we turn to the Word of God. Two thousand years can distance us from the person of Jesus Christ even more than the formula $E = mc^2$ can distance us from the not-too-long-deceased Einstein. And yet we claim to know our faith, to know our God, to know Jesus Christ, revealed in words of no fewer than two thousand years standing.

Has it ever occurred to you why Christians claim to 'know' Jesus Christ so confidently? And why they regard the privileged moment of knowing as that moment when together they repeat a story which begins 'The night before he died . . .'? It is because, as we know from the TV historical productions, stories involve people, and truth ceases to be cold facts, but seems inescapably bound up with love. We don't worship a fact – 'This is my Body'. We worship the person who, in the story, said more and did more: 'This is my body which will be given up for you'.

I want to make a plea: to learn and to teach in a Catholic school is a unique personal act if we will accept the Gospel vision of life. That is why a Catholic school must seek to celebrate the Eucharist and repeat the story if it is to remain a place where the truth will be known in love. When we hear Paul say to his beloved Philippians: 'I thank my God for you' (Philippians 3:1), we know that he must have also said this at the Eucharist. He keeps linking truth and love: 'God is my witness that I tell the truth when I say that my deep feeling for you all comes from the heart of Jesus Christ himself'. And when John repeats Jesus' words at the Last Supper, they are words that come from one who seeks the truth in love: 'Keep those you have given me true to your name'.

To really know Jesus is not simply to respond to the fact of his presence with a nod or a bend. It is to be moved by love to want to love him in return. A school community exists to make Jesus known and loved. To each youngster I would want to say that your parents are not simply biological facts, but are two people whose deep love brought you into existence and now sustains you. Likewise, your teachers are not just educational necessities but people who, believe it or not, love you, thank God for you, pray for you. And if you can point to times when apparently they do not seem to love you in this way, then you are simply pointing to the mystery of sin in their lives – a mystery that you too share in. However, because we proclaim Jesus as God's love for all mankind, that sin of yours and theirs cannot withstand the love of God. A school community or a home that personally knows and loves Jesus will overcome sin and misunderstanding by expressing reconciliation.

I said initially that learning and teaching are personal acts. A boy who was completing his secondary education at our school once said to me in conversation: 'Father, if you are speaking to the school community, please talk about attaining goals and sticking to your purpose'. That was heartfelt personal advice from one who now felt, and rightly so, satisfaction at having achieved a goal, having persevered for a purpose. I believe I have done here what he asked. To complete one's education is a worthy goal; maybe just to survive five or six years of secondary school is praiseworthy; it will be a desirable goal to find a suitable occupation following it, and to find and stand by a partner in life. But to know and to love Jesus Christ through it all is the supreme goal. It is in Christ that we find the answer to the deepest longings of the heart, to the fullness of our hopes. It is in the Gospel that we find the meaning of life and see clearly the meaning and dignity of the human person. So to that boy and to many others I say: know and love Jesus and you will know and love God. Know and love God and you will know and love the person you are, and others for who they are. Not even your petty sins can cloud your purpose; no misfortune can dull your happiness.

Peer group pressure

We have all heard of peer group pressure. Funny, isn't it, that a phrase like this takes on such sinister overtones. We believe, far too easily, that peer group pressure is a label one applies to young people who have done something wrong. I take issue with the assumptions behind such a belief.

'Peer' has an interesting pedigree in the English language. A mere century after it came into the language in the thirteenth century, the world already had noble connections. Still today, a peer in the British Parliament is a person of considerable standing. But that aside, in normal parlance one's peer is one's equal, age notwithstanding! Adults have peers too. Let's not restrict the term to adolescents alone.

'Pressure' is a word which of itself is morally neutral. Unfortunately the complexities of twentieth-century living often make pressure a state of harassment, undue concern and worry. But it can also be a state of support, positive persuasion – even ministry to one another. It can be a force for good rather than one for evil.

And 'group'? We live in the world of the psychological man today, where the value of human relationships is supposedly understood far more deeply than ever before. We seem, nevertheless, to distrust the group process, fear it, label it as either an inert, conforming mass or a reactionary minority. Yes, even a 'pressure group'!

Ministry, community growth, support. These are the 'peer group pressures', positively understood, of the faith community. Antioch, that current Catholic youth movement sweeping the country, is peer ministry in action. Young people working for young people – it is a concept we cannot do without.

One doesn't have to read much of Don Bosco's life story to realize not only how naturally sociable he was, but also how creatively distilled this natural urge into group experiences of a formative kind. Group experiences have clear educational value in that they:

1 presuppose free participation;
2 are an authentic activity of young people;
3 stress sensitivity in the service of one's neighbour;
4 bring about a union of aim and commitment with the educator who has a role to play as animator of the experience.

Group experiences may also have clear religious aims in that they:

1 introduce a definite influence of the faith into the daily life of the member;
2 provide a vision of the future which is linked to the Christian virtue of hope;
3 see the fulfilling of one's duty as a religious task;
4 assist individuals to discern their true calling in life;
5 inculcate generous, even heroic, service of one's neighbour by providing a higher motive;
6 see working together as a basic responsibility arising from one's baptismal calling.

We are faced with the urgency of creating vital models of youth association. Pope John Paul II offered this pressing invitation when he spoke to young people gathered in St Peter's Square on 5 May 1979. He has since repeated it many times in many nations, Australia included:

It is not a question of creating militant expressions deprived of ideal impetus and based on the force of numbers, but of animating real communities, instilled with the spirit of kindness, mutual respect and service, and above all made compact by the same faith and by one unique hope . . .

Sorry, the lights just changed

Would a warm Galilean Sunday afternoon be so much different from Melbourne in the summertime? I do not think much imagination would be needed to produce a Sermon on the Mount or a Simon and Andrew fishing in a lake out amidst the mesa-like hills where the town of Sunbury is situated. Sunbury is the home of 'Rupertswood', one of the grand old schools of the nation.

Picture, then, just such a Sunday, and pairs of young disciples sent out around the village on an errand; tunic-clad and sandal-shod, minus haversack and bread and, rather unGospel-like, not only with coppers for their purses but armed with tins and money bags for just that purpose – to beg and scrounge for the regular Doorknock Appeal. There is something distinctly evangelical, I feel, about the whole scene . . . 'If any place does not welcome you, and people refuse to listen to you, as you walk away, shake off the dust from under your feet' (Mark 6:11-12).

It would be interesting indeed to try to recount the mendicant adventures of many a young collector, and to record the responses of a population stripped by a plague that Egypt never knew! Two collectors culled the following responses from their experiences:

'Sorry mate, just bought a new fridge.'
'She'll be right mate.'
'Who? When? Where? Why? No!'
'They just got me.'
'I don't believe in that @ #¢*!'

'Is this for real?'
'Here's 2¢.'
'Stop scabbing.'
'Got no money left.'
'Sorry mate, just had a baby.'
'Sorry, I just got married.'
'It's too hard to get the cash out.'
'Sorry, the lights just changed.'

Collecting for the Red Cross, or for any worthy cause, might have been the closest to a missionary endeavour that many a student thinks he has achieved. Could be, but I would dispute this. 'Are you prepared to witness to your Christian Faith?' suggests one question in the enrolment process, and the young hopeful answers affirmatively, with a twinge of a doubt as to what that might mean in practice.

Life as a student in a Catholic school is full of missionary opportunities, and it does not even require a tour of the village to achieve it. The harvest is right in the students' midst and the call to labour in that harvest is clear – directly requested or modulated through a variety of persons and situations.

Action Groups in Catholic schools have featured prominently in both the 'call' and the response to it. Such groups have been an integral part of Salesian education since Don Bosco's own 'Happy Community' (an action group that he formed around himself while still at school). They have continued to exist according to the piety and the ecclesiology of the age.

We live at a time when models or paradigms are 'in' as a way of analyzing and understanding phenomena. Schools are often viewed from the business model (wrongly I believe, for schools are not businesses). The Church has been viewed from several models over the centuries. In what sense is an Action Group a mini-school or Church?

One approach might be to consider the school from the viewpoint of family – the model is productive and close to the heart of Don Bosco. An Action Group, according to this model, has a family structure with all that entails in terms of brotherly support, paternal direction and mutual tolerance. Despite its appeal, the family model is not adequate to describe the thrust and drive of the Action Group.

So we turn to the Scriptures and the models of Church that have developed from them in the Christian tradition.

There is the *servant* model. Church in service of humanity. But the danger of defining the group in terms of its service to humanity is that the action may be more than human action. Benevolent atheists can collect money for the Red Cross as efficiently as a young Catholic student might. Besides, 'servant' in a school community has many connotations which make it less fruitful as a model.

Church has often been understood as proclamation: the *herald* model. Again, I doubt that this would help. The Church has a clear message to preach from the housetops both in season and out of season. Such clarity, either of purpose or content, is rare in adolescence and human respect is a powerful obstacle to proclamation. It is an adolescent failing *par excellence*.

No, the model that best suits the Action Group is right back there in Galilee where this reflection began. Pope John Paul II himself clearly developed such a model as his view of the twentieth century Church – the model of the disciples.

> It is the community of the disciples each of whom in a different way – at times very consciously and consistently, at times not very consciously and consistently – is following Christ.
>
> (Redemptor Hominis n. 21)

Here is an insight delightfully appropriate to the adolescent group. John Paul knows young people so well! They are at times consistent and at times not!

We may debate that the Master wished to found a Church. We cannot debate that he formed a band of disciples, and that his call was 'Follow me', and that there wasn't a perfect one amongst them. And it was one of Don Bosco's key evangelical insights that he followed the Master in just this way too, incessantly inviting whoever would accept the call to a closer association, to action, and to a probing of self that would slowly eliminate the inconsistencies. 'Be you perfect as your heavenly father is perfect' (Matt. 5:48).

Working amongst young people in these groups is a rare

Gospel experience. How true and human is Mark's emphasis on the slowness of the disciples to grasp Jesus' teaching about service and suffering. Yet in common they accepted that it was good to gather in unity, converse intimately with the Master, and accept the adventure of following Jesus in the ever-changing situation of the here-and-now.

Life today must learn to cope with change and conflict; it must also seek consensus where it can. 'Servants' are likely to seek consensus through submission. That does not wash today. 'Heralds' may achieve it through noisy dominance. That will not wash either. But 'Disciples' stand resolutely against the tide or the times by modestly accepting that they have not yet arrived, are still open to correction, but are on the way to a full and blessed life.

Such disciples are the members of the Action Groups, we hope. They are not daunted when the lights change. They will get you on the way back!

The nest or the cage?

Somehow the very mention of discipline brings clouds to the horizon of adolescent outlook. The word sounds sacrilegious in the company of an unholy racket in the corridor between classes. And then there is that peculiar quality of the young which is not irreverence, quite, but the next best thing. One may well ask, with tongue-in-cheek: 'O Discipline, where is thy sting?'

Discipline and education might seem yoked together like the good old horse and carriage . . . or love and marriage. But what kind of discipline for what kind of education? It is an important question. Could it be that traditional Western education, owing so much to Plato, or more recently to Rousseau, or Dewey, has taken the intellectual path where discipline is simply order imposed for the purpose of instruction? This I would see as the discipline of the cage. Somewhere, somehow, discipline has switched tracks. The word, after all, is recognizably a derivative of 'disciple'. The disciple, at least in the Christian dispensation, is more passionate than pedantic, more catholic than caged, and certainly more at home on the winding paths of Judaea than in the temples of learning at Jerusalem. This is the discipline of the nest.

I have reflected often on the nature of discipline. Disciples are the followers of The Way. I believe we can articulate an understanding of discipline within such a model. There is a famous film on the life of Don Bosco which shows him leading a long line of youthful delinquents out the front door of a prison – alone and without warders – for a day's outing. From the cage to the nest; Don Bosco's 'nest' where discipline was virtually self-imposed in a climate of love.

Young people do things passionately: they run, jump, kick footballs or catch frogs with the same undiminishing energy and commitment to the task. Don Bosco saw that discipline must adapt to that sort of energy. He also understood, intuitively, that true discipline was the meeting point between two free agents. This is not a new idea; it is at the heart of the Gospel's perspective on conversion. Discipline, *à la* Don Bosco, is a powerful amalgam of Scripture, Christian tradition and good old common sense. From men such as St Paul and St Francis de Sales, Don Bosco had distilled a formula for discipline: reason, religion and loving kindness. When Don Bosco taught maths, he would introduce algebra with the formula $a + b - c$, then explain it thus: *Allegro* (happy) plus *Buono* (good) minus *Cattivo* (bad). Herein lay his whole approach to teaching and learning: happiness and goodness with the positive elimination of evil. 'Let the boys run and jump and make as much noise as they will', he would explain to ruffled colleagues, 'so long as they do not sin'.

Our English word 'school' could well be traced to its roots also, since discipline is usually associated with school. It has come down to us, via Latin (*schola*) from the Greek *skole* which means . . . wait for it . . . leisure! Now, in our twentieth century mentality, the opposite to leisure has become work. I would suggest that for Don Bosco, its opposite was not work but laziness, inactivity. School, amongst other things, was for him a place of intense activity. Active youngsters need little imposed discipline. Consider discipline in the context of a game; we all know how effective that can be. Very often it is self-imposed. It was in the games and leisure moments of the young person that Don Bosco saw his 'Reason', rather than in the intellectual debates of the scholars. In the natural exuberant experiences of the young, cheerfulness and order are of the same ilk. In young people Don Bosco had found, I believe, the 'little way' of perfection through ordinary pursuits; simple, commonplace and so loved by the young.

Yet Don Bosco's greatest insights into discipline lay not so much in the discovery of the principle of reason seen through the nature of a child. Life was not all fun and games, and attention to duty, along with a measured seriousness when it was required, was just as much a part of his understanding. It is a balance that he found in the saint whom he chose as patron of his fledgling society – St Francis de Sales. It is also a balance to be found in another great follower of The Way, Paul of Tarsus. Both saints were forceful, even impatient and tempestuous by nature, as was Don Bosco himself. Yet both controlled their lives with the sweetness of Christ.

St Paul's sanctity lay in his ability to be all things to all people. It would be easy to quote his dictums of love, wherein he rises, at times, to superb lyrical heights. 'Religion', for Paul, had more substance than that! He could also speak of a God who would sometimes chastise to show his love. Paul himself could fulminate with the wrath of God. We flinch as we hear Paul word-whip the Corinthian revellers out of their drunken orgies, or castigate those who would lead the weak astray. We learn from Paul that 'Religion' must face the problem of recalcitrant human nature with prodigious energy.

And thank God for Francis! Maybe the Protestants of the Swiss cantons of his time were not as unruly as the Corinthians. Certainly we do not find the Pauline barbs or invectives in the writings of the gentle Bishop of Geneva. Yet his arrival amidst broken crosses, burnt-down churches and shouting must have sorely tempted a man who was no mean swordsman and hot-headed to boot. Christlike kindness won the day, but not without a due measure of work and temperance.

In short, discipline takes on a fresh perspective when

viewed through the eyes of faith, and when this is allied to the firm belief that childhood and adolescence are stages of faith rather than difficult periods to be surmounted.

The school community

The school community makes an interesting community to study because it reflects very well the nature of community in contemporary society. If we go back to primitive times, we find that communities were made up of groups sharing much in common. Today, this rarely happens with large-scale communities. Towns and cities comprise neighbours who by and large don't know one another, who may even be afraid of one another, and whose mobility makes for a grand mixture of people and ways of life. A school reflects this comparatively disintegrated society.

Nevertheless, the human being desires companionship, by which I mean working together, sharing time and place; human beings also desire friendship, by which I mean a sharing of common vision and concern. Inasmuch as we desire these forms of association, we seek mutual interest groups. School students are, through parental choice, companions in the sense described above. If they are to be friends, much work has to be done to help create the conditions for common vision and concern.

There is much ignorance, even in a society supposedly sophisticated about such things, of what makes community. Putting people together because they simply get on or share a similar ideal does not of itself make community – witness the problems that married life encounters when based solely on such criteria. Something more is needed. The problems are exacerbated when we realize that a youngster between the ages of twelve and eighteen is going through the process of establishing that sort of strong ego-centre (quite necessary to a well-integrated adult future) which makes community building difficult. How is it possible, we might ask, to fulfil St Paul's hope that there 'be no competition amongst you, no conceit; everybody is to be self-effacing. Always consider the other person to be better than yourself so that nobody thinks of his own interests first' (Philippians 2:3-4)?

At a Catholic school we profess to be working towards a Christian community. This is a revealed notion, not arrived at through sociology or psychology. It has two basic tenets: 'As the Father has loved me, so I have loved you. Remain in my love', and 'Love one another as I have loved you'. Both are to be found in Chapter 15 of St John's Gospel. The first is a reminder that the initiative is God's – his grace, his Spirit forms this community which abides. The second is a reminder to us of how we must act. It has to be translated into practical things like accepting others in their limitations, helping them to belong, seeing beyond oneself or one's group to others' needs. The Church continually strives to be such a community called together by the Word, lived in communion and expressing itself in service of one another and the world.

A school is more than a Church community. It is also an educational community. There was a time when education was very much an expression of individual management. That is rarely so today. Those responsible for the administration and management of schools, State or denominational, are now seen as animating forces binding the endeavours of all together, rather than as instruments of total control.

For my part, I would like to offer a third motivation for creating a school community, drawn from my own background and experience as a son of Don Bosco. A school has the possibility of being a 'family' type of community which will result in the complete formation of the individual. To be such it requires an intense and bright environment of participation of young and old alike, and especially the loving, sympathetic, active and animating presence of educators amongst the pupils.

What does such a community – using all three motivations – offer to the administrative structure and processes of the Catholic school? At least the following:

1   Profound human relationships. More frequent contact between ourselves, more rather than less communication; systematic rather than desultory communication. Relation-

ships within such a community can be more than cordial, based as they are on a sense of working in common. In addition to being the basis for a strong professional relationship, the community offers a pastoral rapport between all those who are trying to grow in faith together.

2   A reality to which people adhere through some deeply felt choice. A pastoral educative community is more than just a participation technique. Here I am talking about a sense of belonging which can only come from a genuinely felt acceptance of what the community is on about. A Catholic school, for example, claims to proclaim and bear witness to the Gospel. It does far more than simply teach, promote human advancement, or engage in a worthwhile social service activity.

3   A clear sense of identity. There are many educational philosophies around. Can a Catholic school offer a clear sense of identity? I believe it can if it takes up the notion of education as a well-elaborated project involving definable ends, style, areas and competencies.

Dedication

Most authors have put a dedicatory comment at the beginning of a book. I have chosen to put mine last. This book has been a result of continual reflection on experience, a listening, not just to one song but to many. A principal of a Catholic school regards this as one of his or her most fundamental tasks in the overall responsibility of educational and pastoral leadership.

Circumstances, and I have no doubt it was the Lord who 'arranged' all of these, drew me gradually into the circle of those who educated and expressed their vision of the Gospel according to the lines traced out by the life and work of St John Bosco. I have tried to express and share publicly a vision (another fundamental task of the principal) which is the result of my Salesian experience, in such a way as to say to people: this is not an exclusive vision. It is open to anyone who can read the Gospel this way and who feels a deep love for the young.

And the interesting thing for me has been, that as I take each experience and reflect on it, I realize that I had known or experienced it long before I had heard of St John Bosco. The fundamental school of my life has been the family, and it was especially from my father that I had learnt, from the earliest moments, what fatherliness was all about. It was not difficult to discover the love of God in that climate.

To Dad, then, especially, I dedicate these pages and thank the Lord daily for the lively example that he has given and continues to give.